Unchained Fixations

Illustrations by

E.R. Schiller

First Printing: 24 July 2020

ISBN: 978-0-578-70441-8

Table of Contents

Author Statement

All artwork in this collection was hand drawn within a span of eight months. Drawing became the lone source of comfort during a tumultuous and lethal period debuting a new decade. With unwavering passion and spiteful determination, I churned out piece after piece, until my fingers ached and my knuckles blistered, the blind stream of hours a superficial casualty of prolonged isolation. A small sacrifice of the corporeal vehicle in a strange and unpredictable life. It could be argued this book is a vain exercise, my third published book in less than one year before the age of twenty-five. It could also be argued this is my declaration against the uncertain, that despite the escalating anxiety and dismal potential of the present, I did what I could within my narrowing circle of existence. This was my fight.

July 2020

I. Unconventional Love Stories

Abstract: Chapter One

This section is devoted to couples and triads of the bizarre and unwieldy. Unrelenting desires that conform to no socially acceptable circumstance. A triumph of attraction over logic, each drawing depicts individuals pulled together through forces as mysterious and unknowable as themselves.

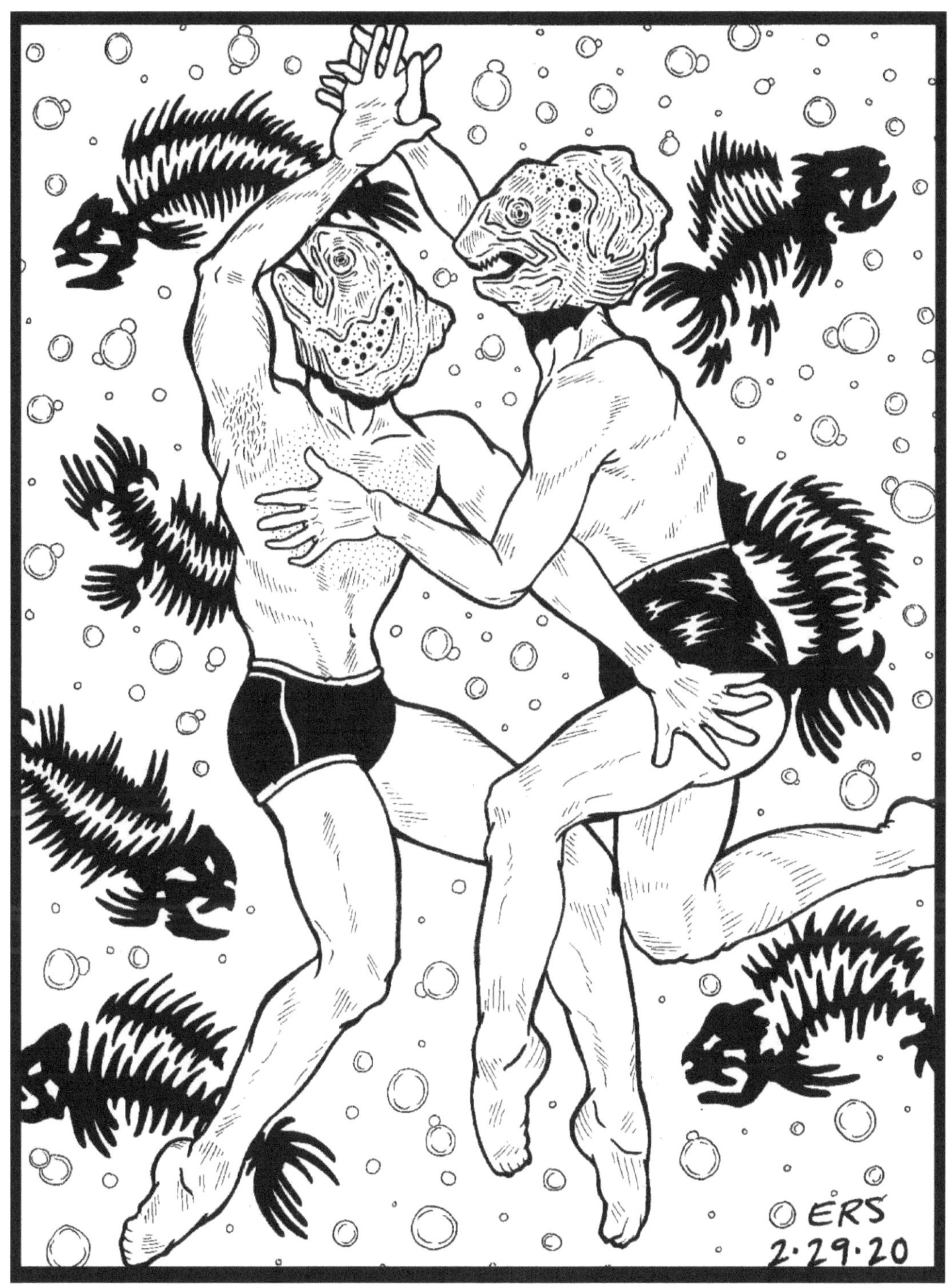

Amphibious Mating Dance

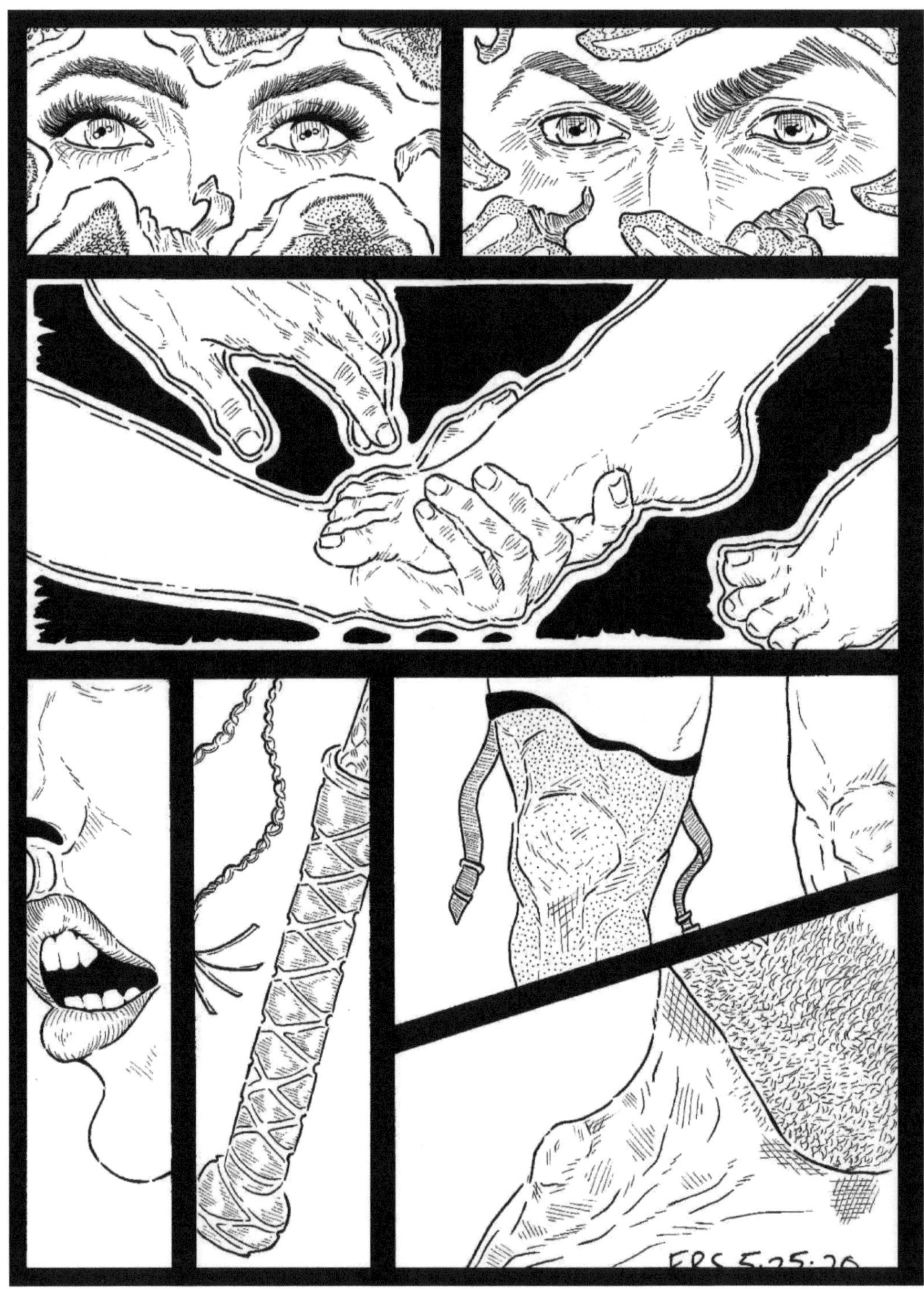

Mutual Agreement

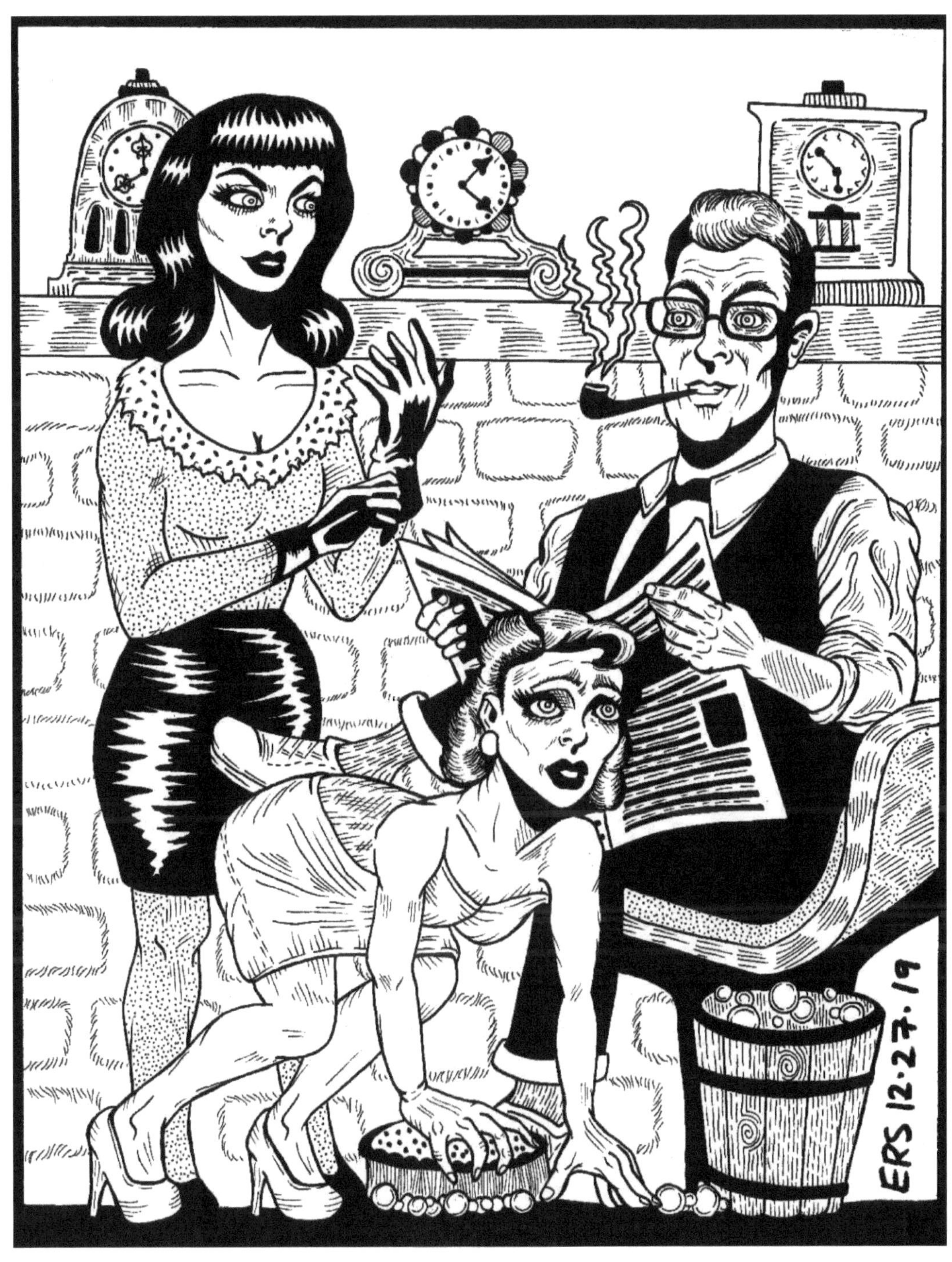

Sunday at Home

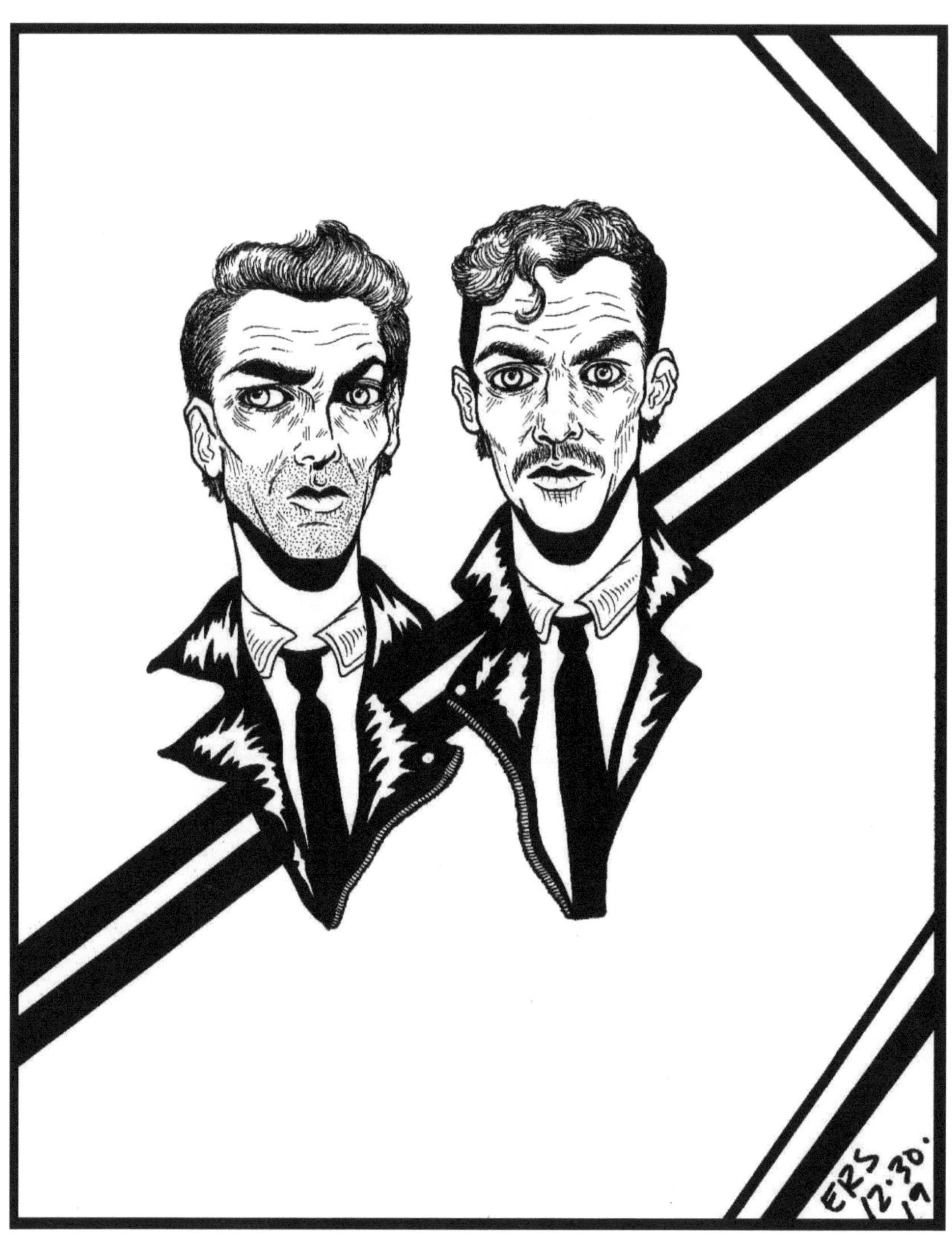

Leather Lovers

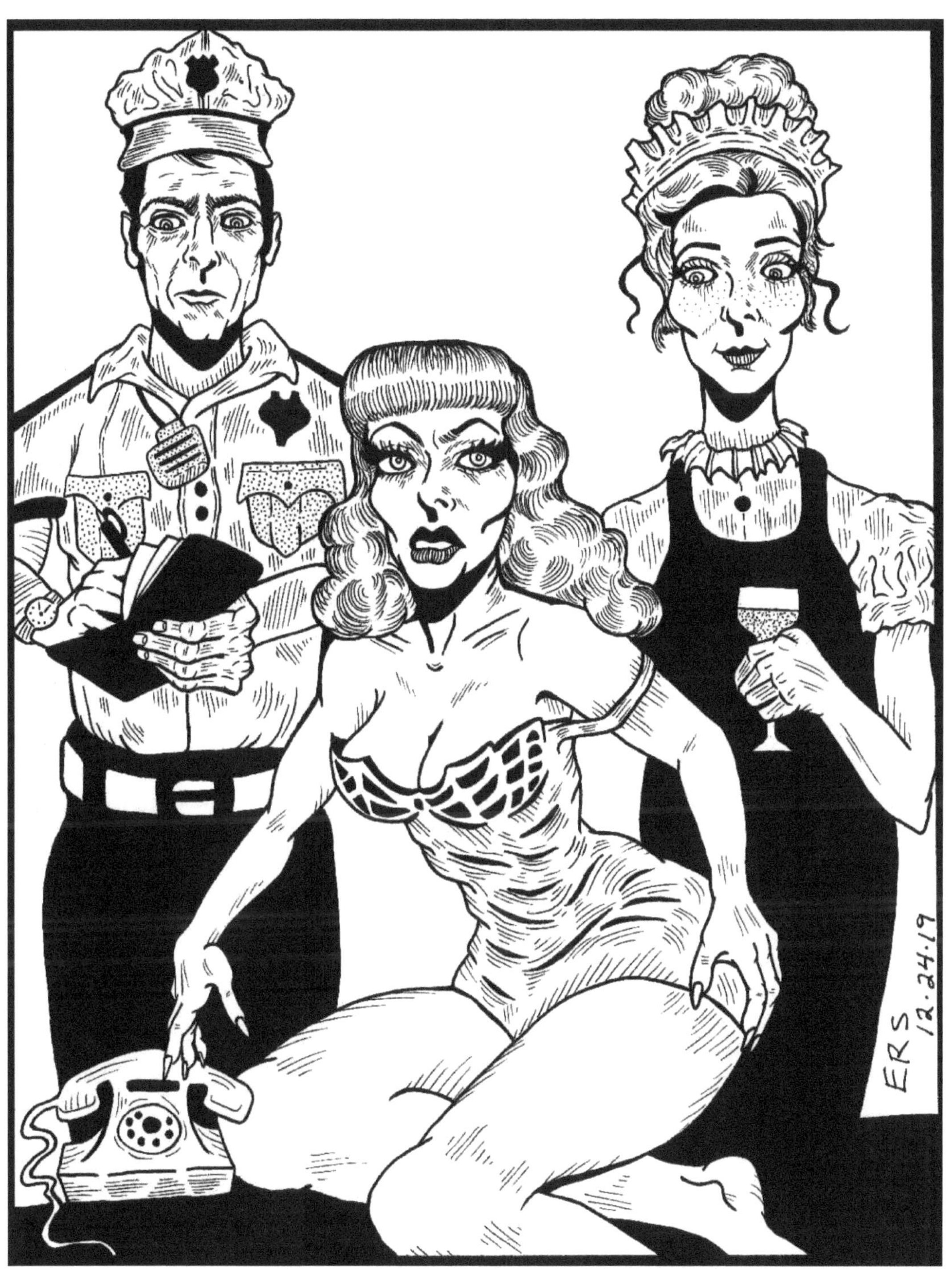

Uncooperative Mistress

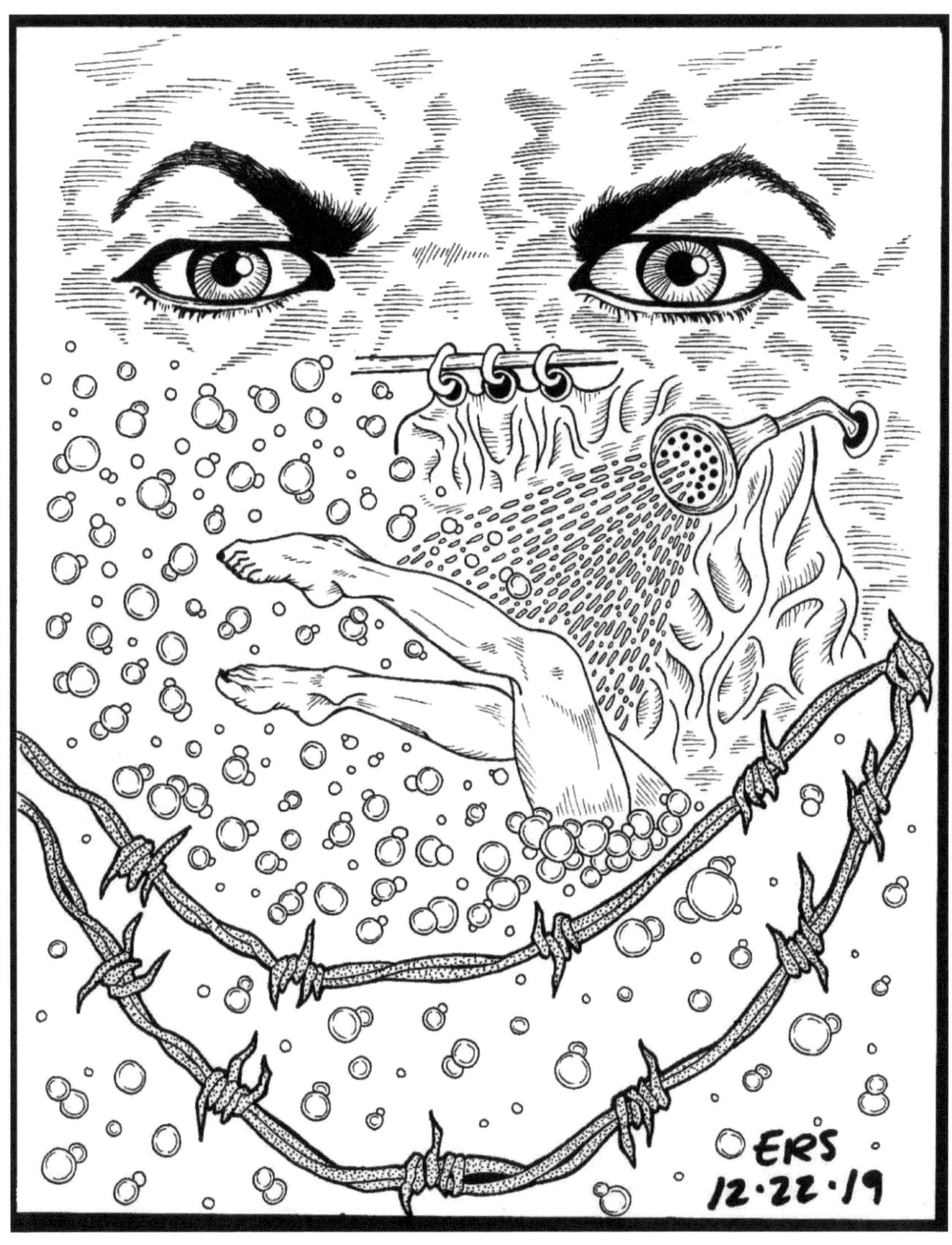

Bubble Bath Demise

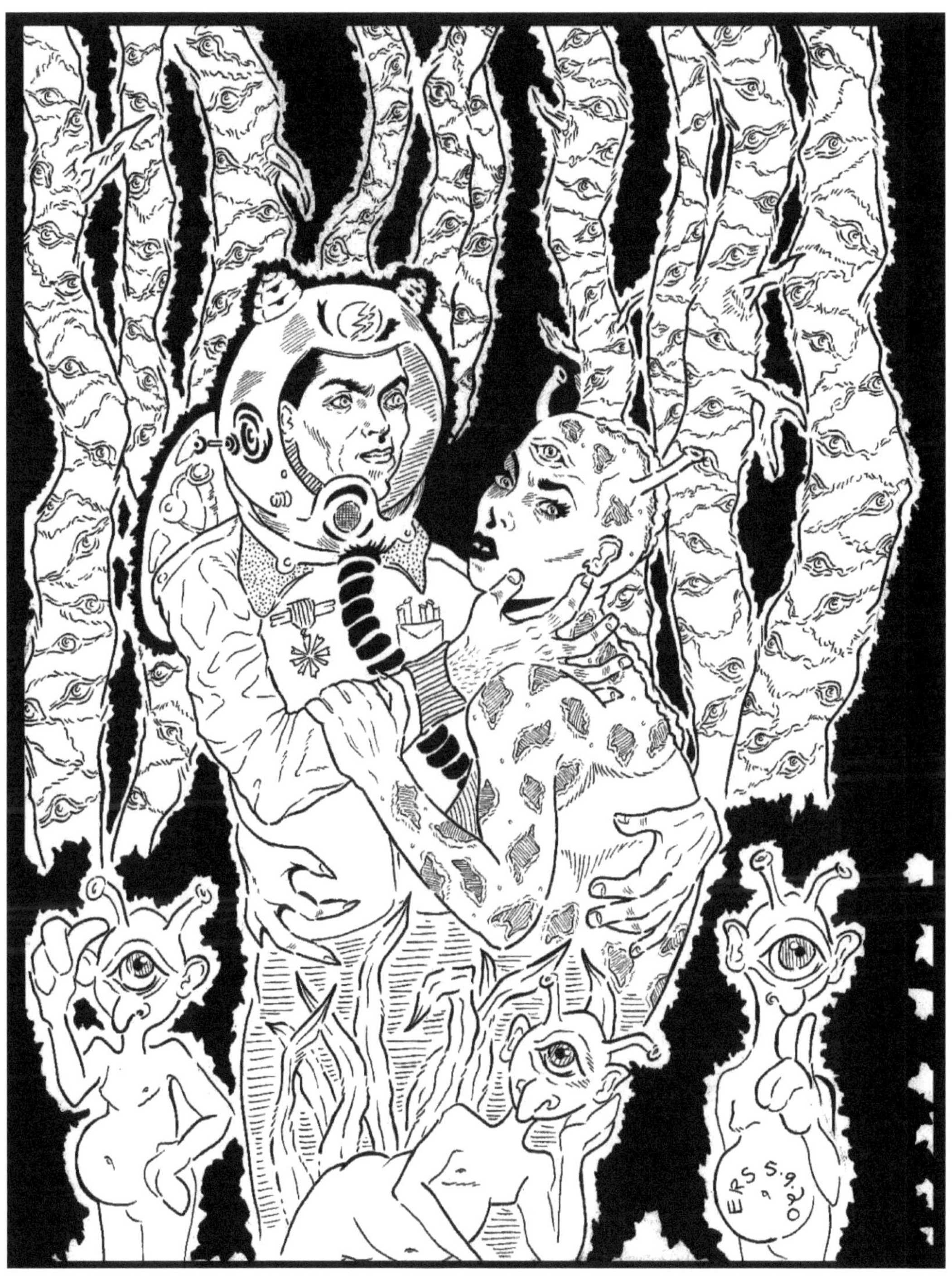

Alien Kiss

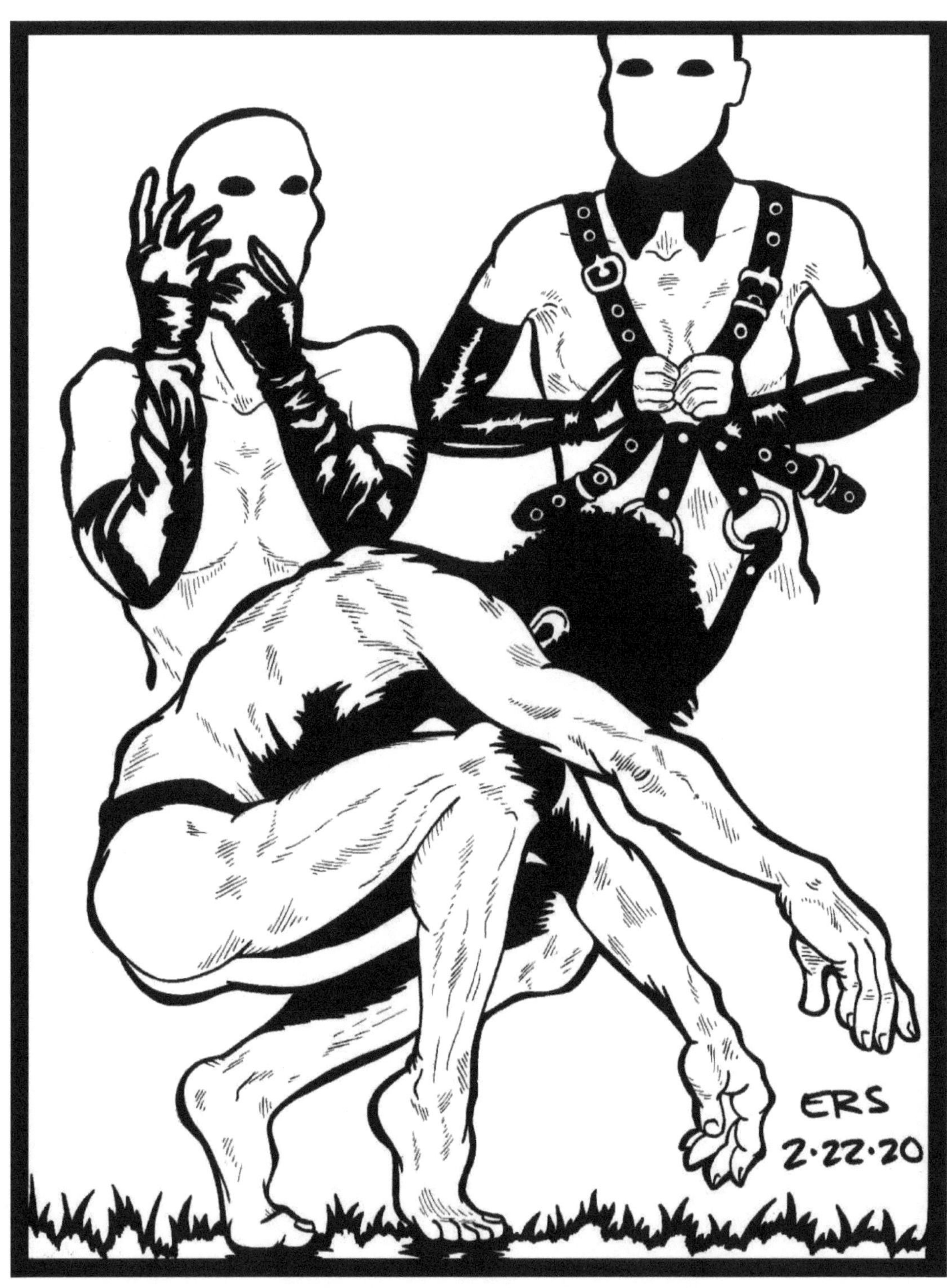

Faceless Tormentors

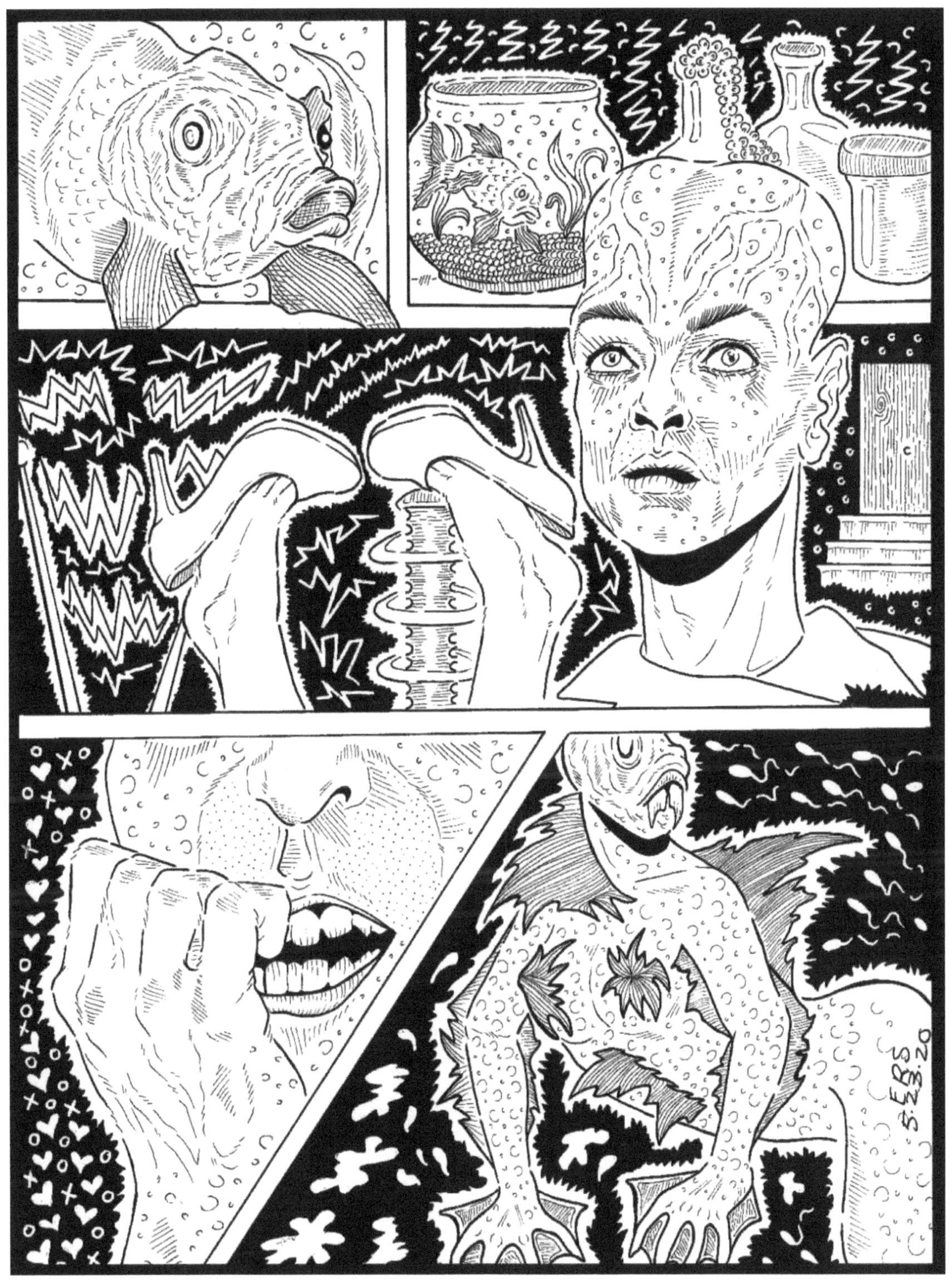

Lab Dreamer

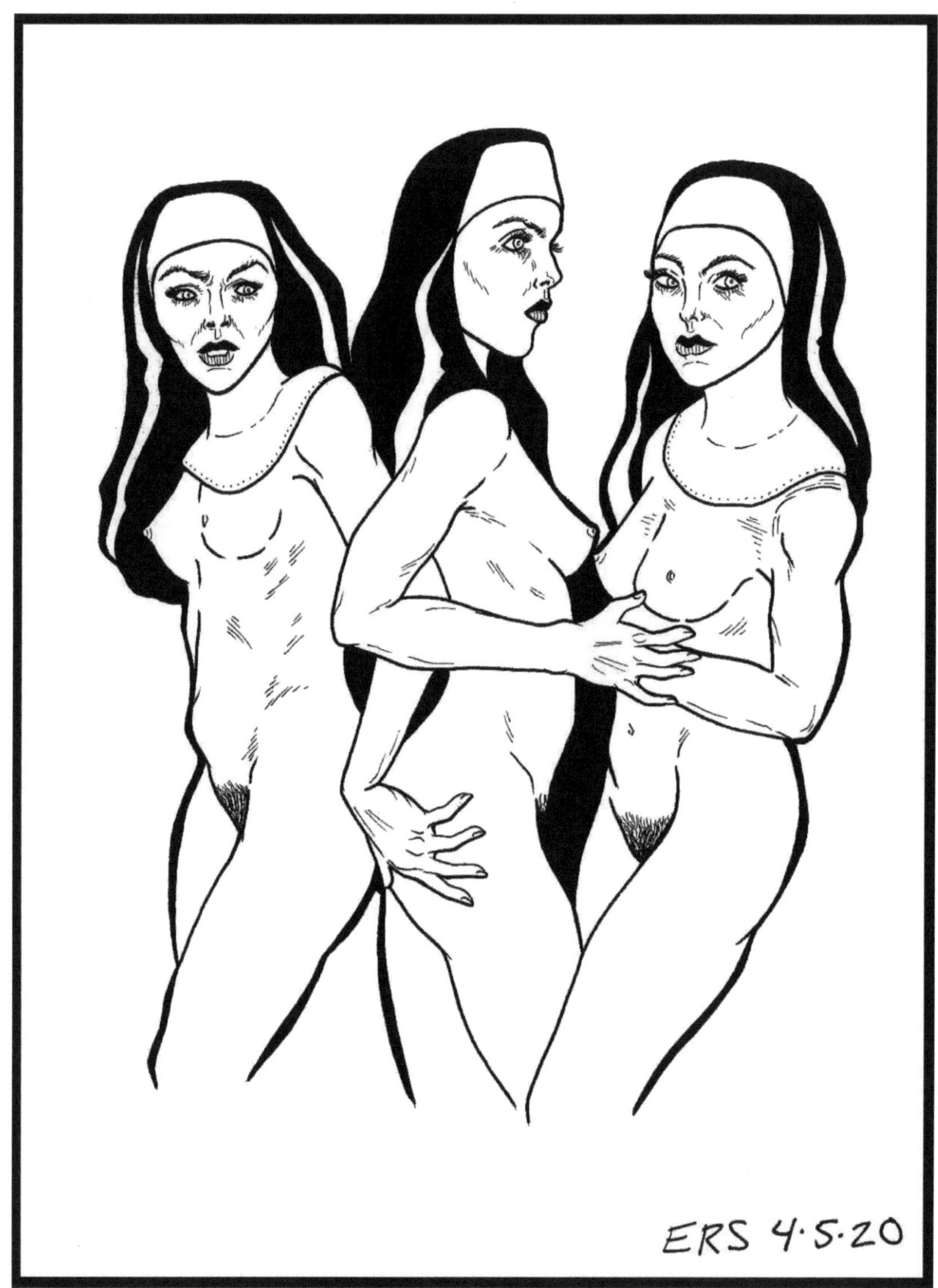

Sweet Trinity

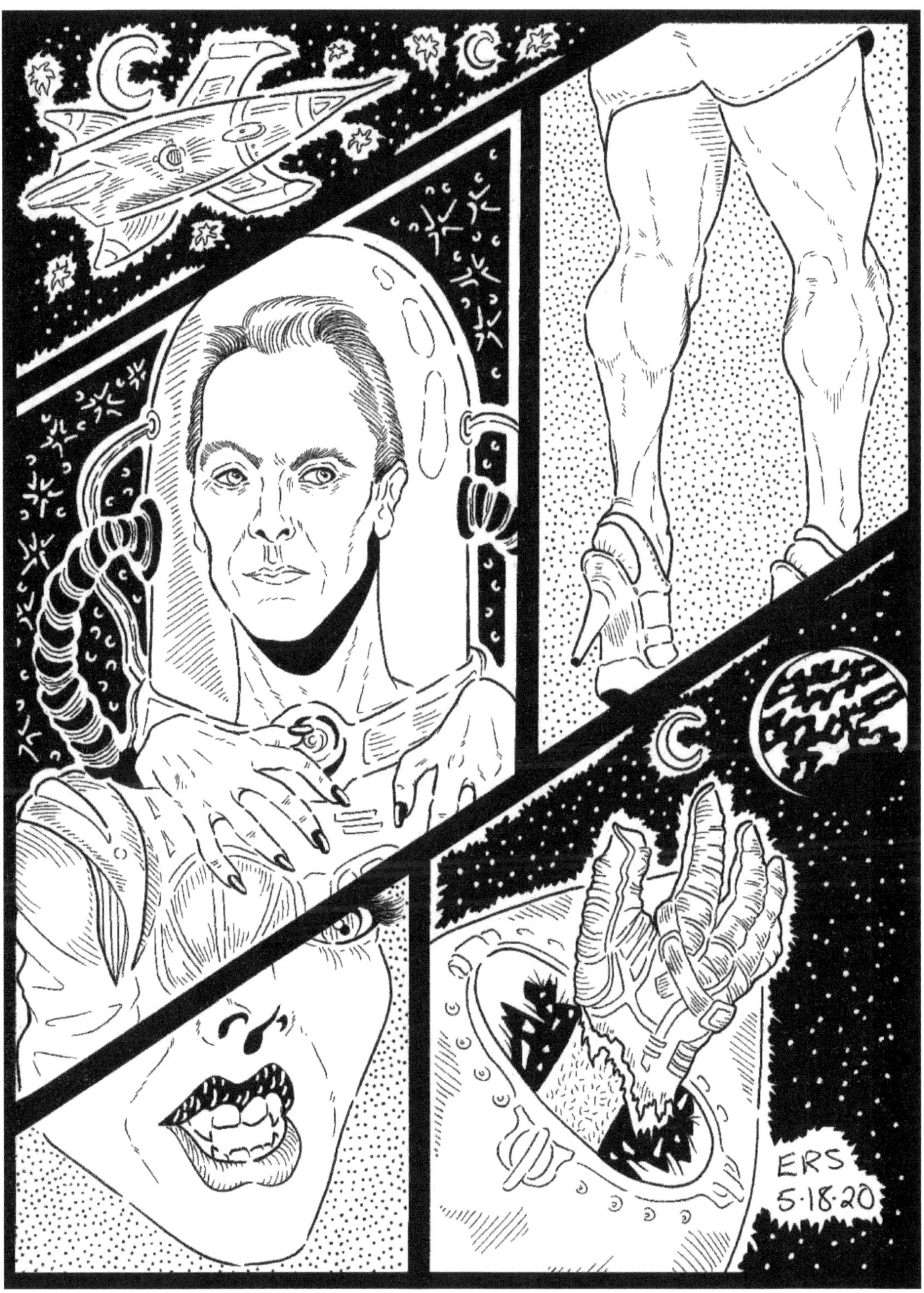

Space Vampire

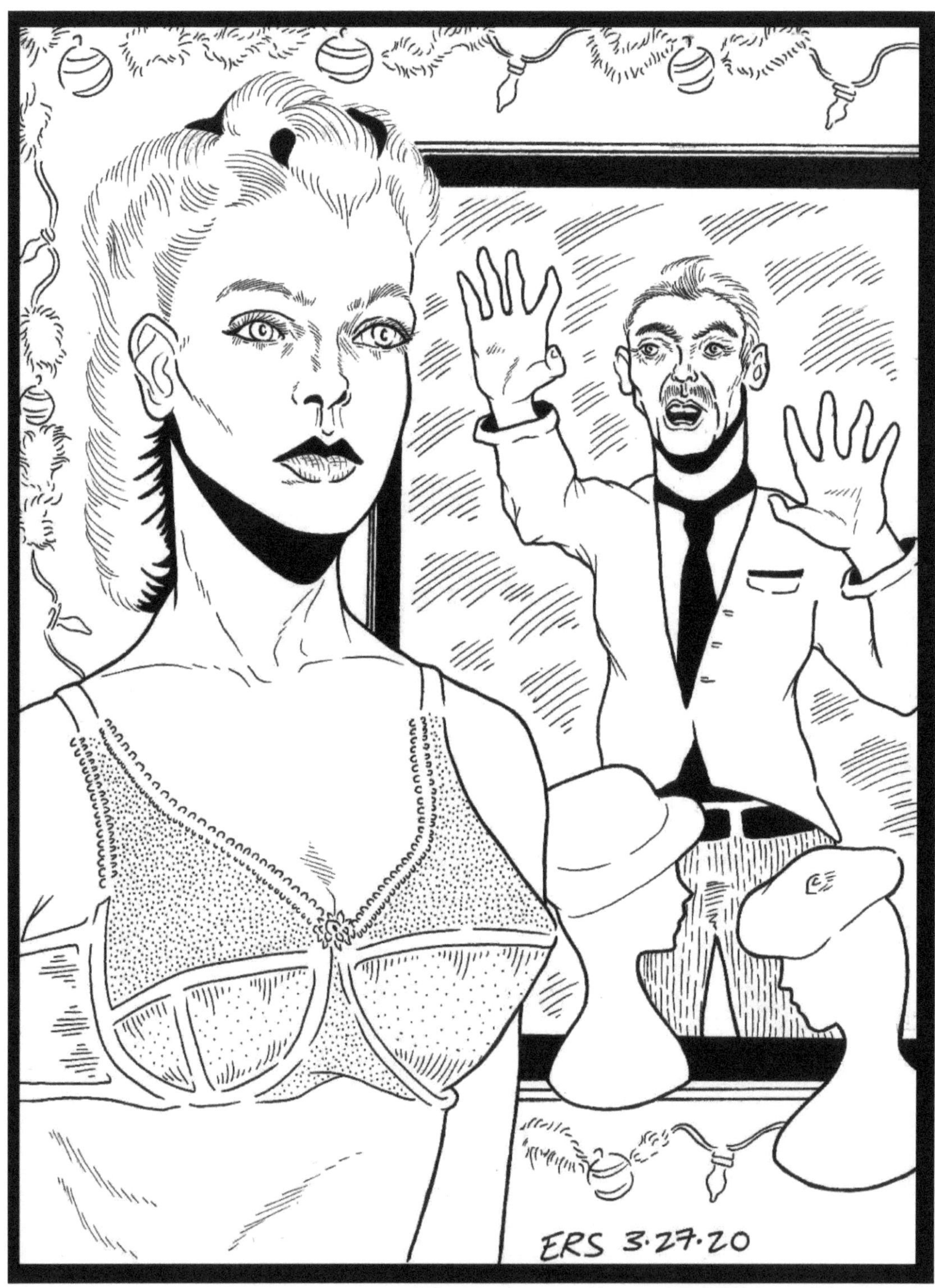

Manic Window Shopper

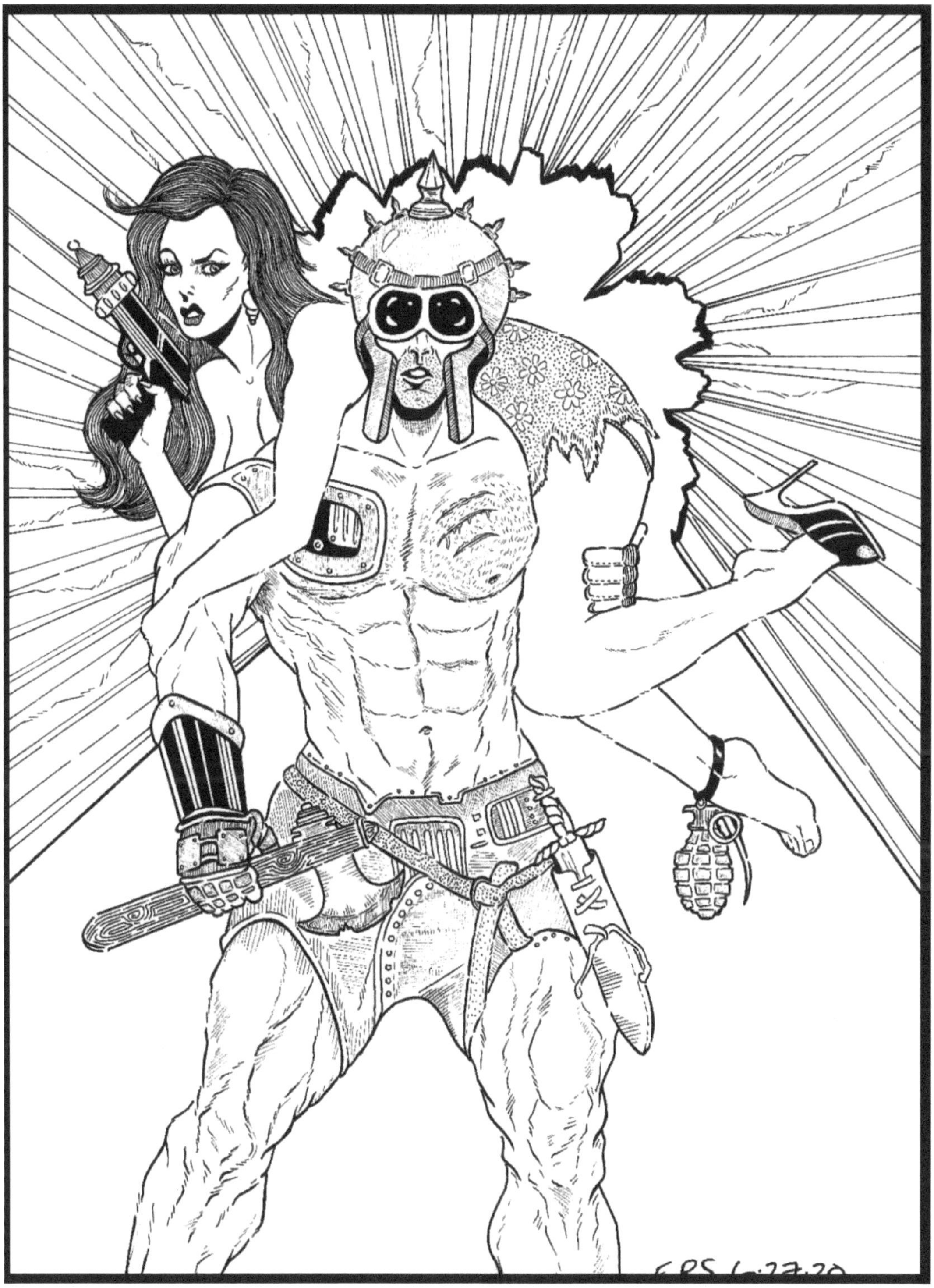

Apocalyptic Team Work

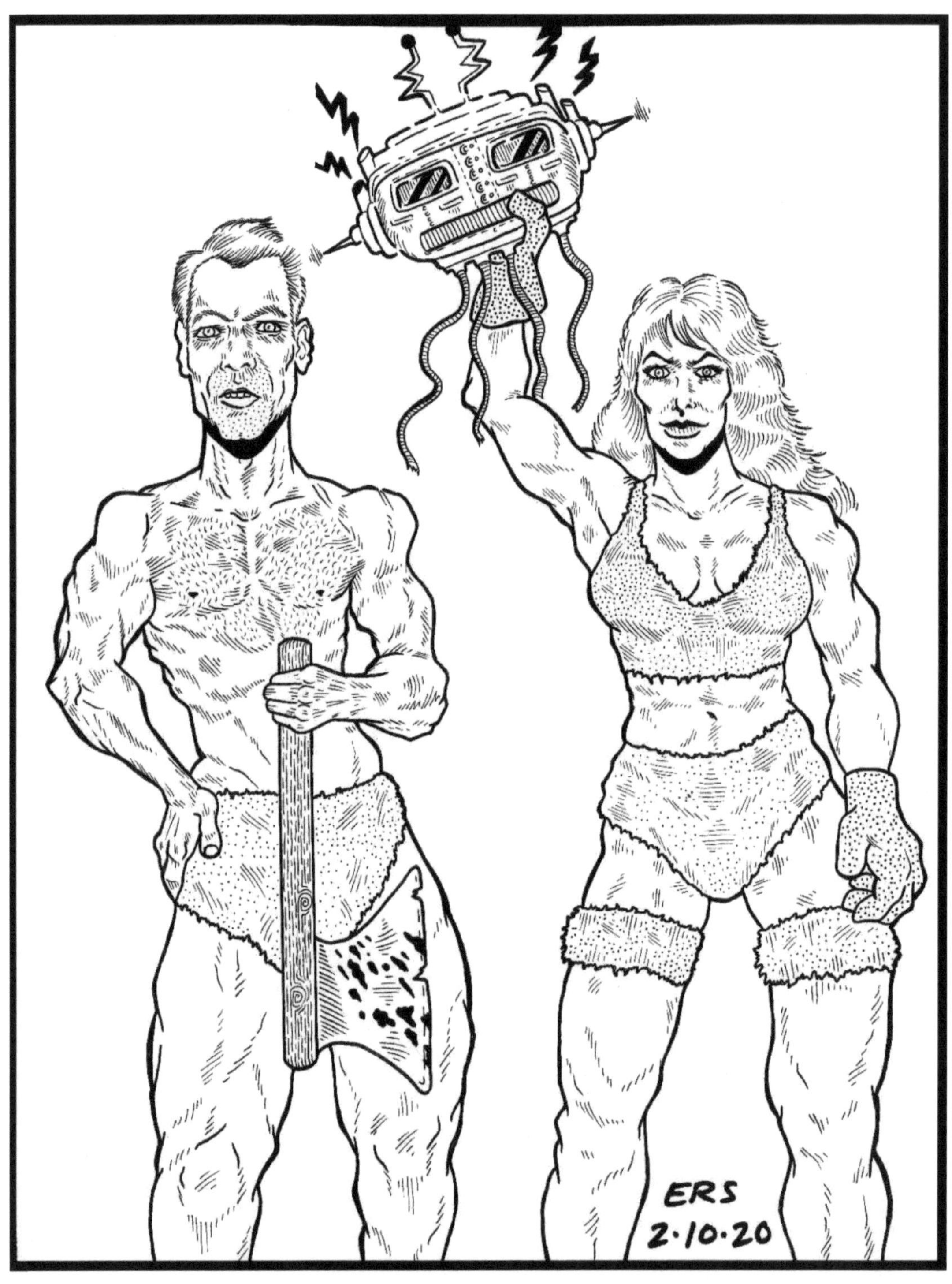

Barbarian v Robot

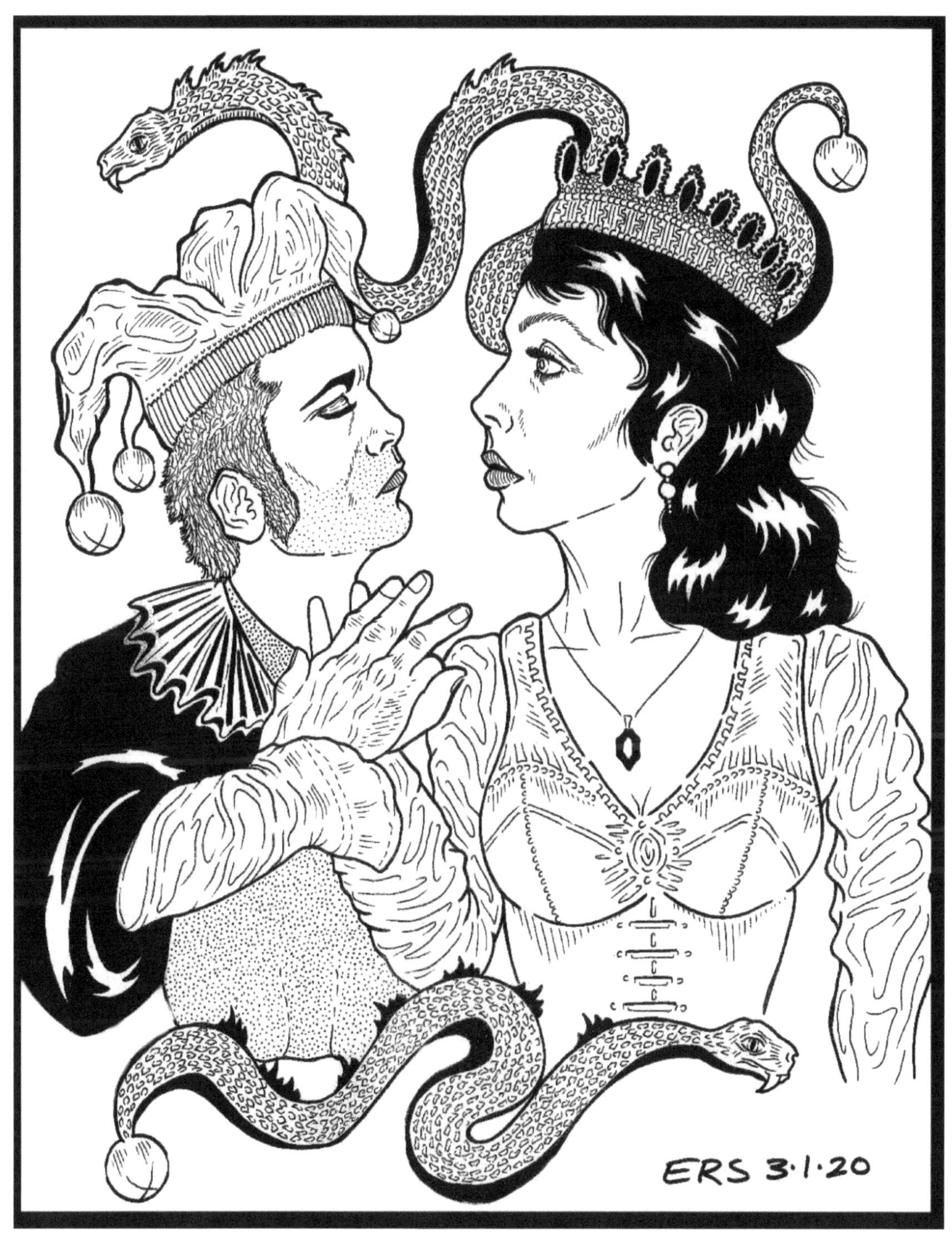

Private Joke

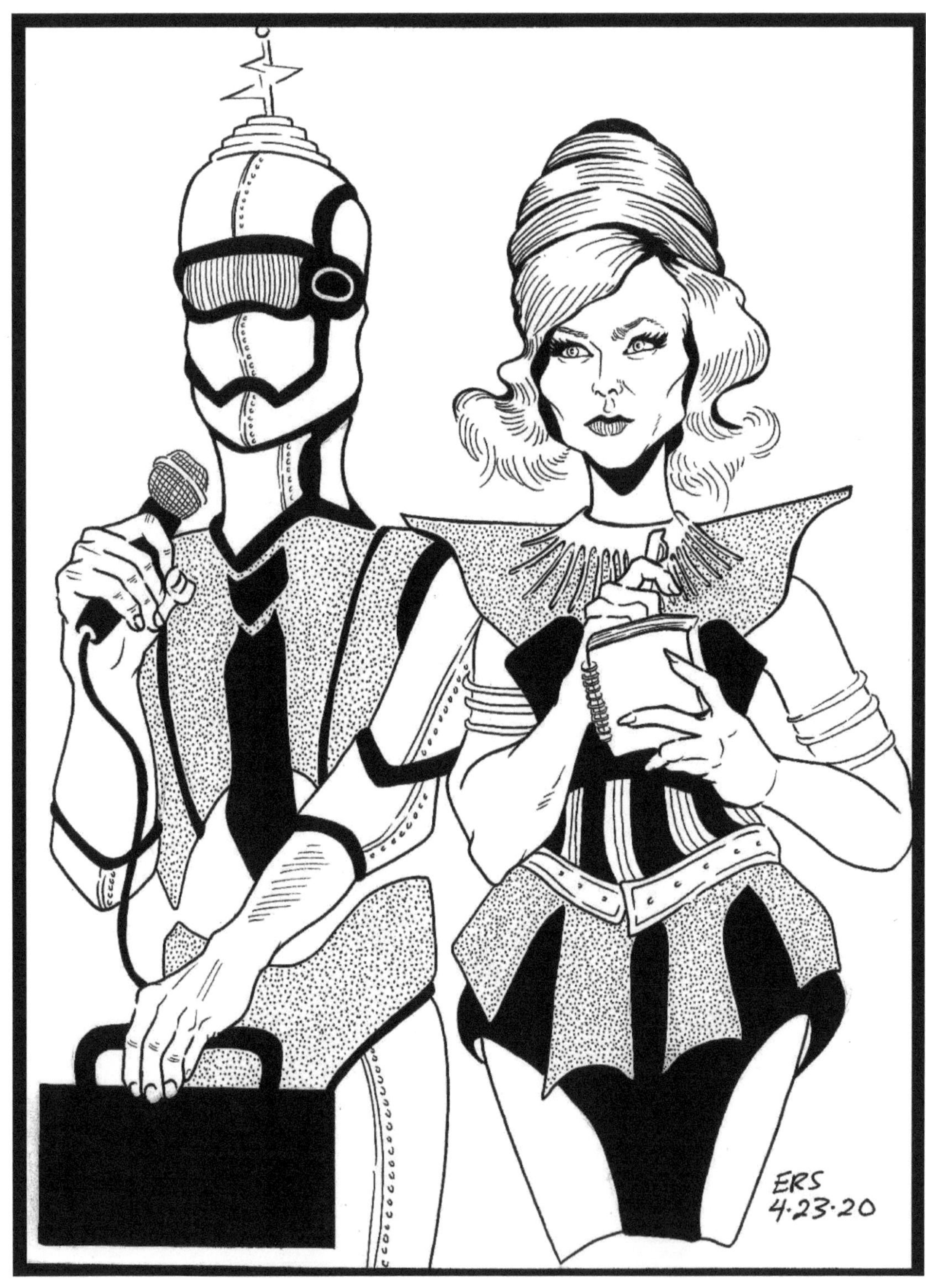

3020 Press Briefing

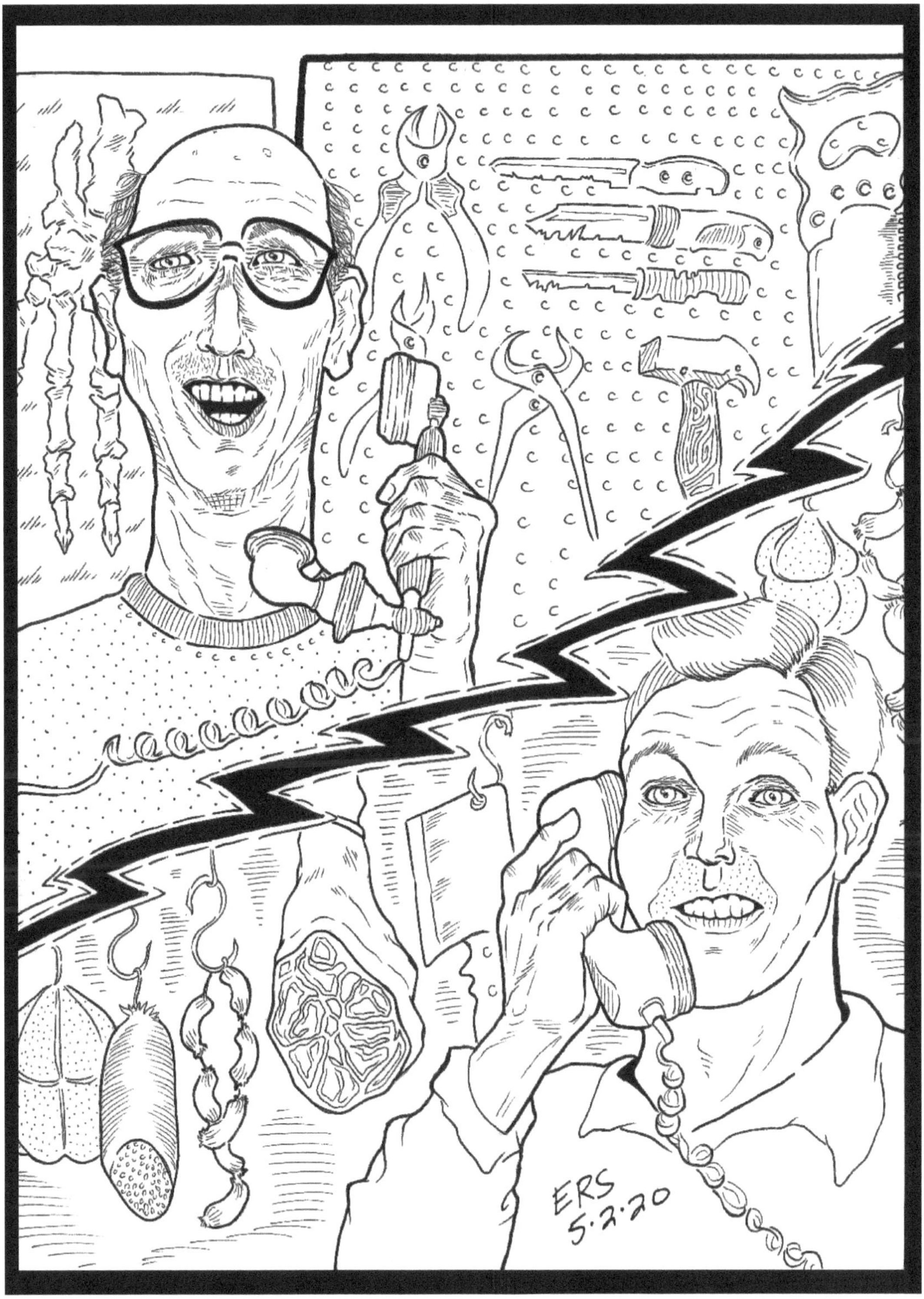

Planning the Big Day

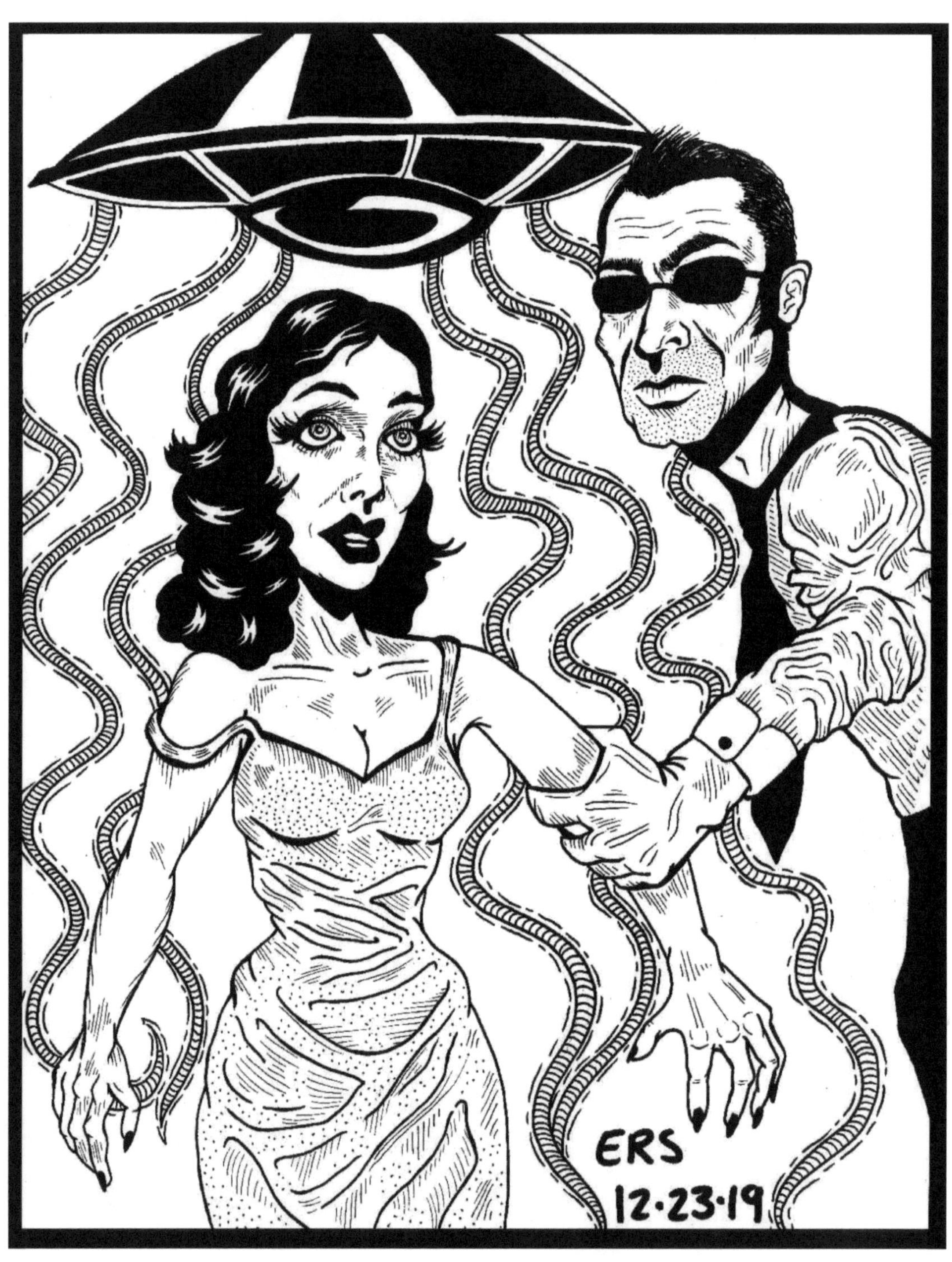

Irresistible Kidnappers

II. Undefeated Female

Abstract: Chapter Two

The following series portrays women participating in unique circumstances. Despite the chaotic or unusual settings they may inhabit or any external entities seizing upon them, they are complex personages authentically engaged with their environment. Their emotions and strength are displayed in fearless exhibition.

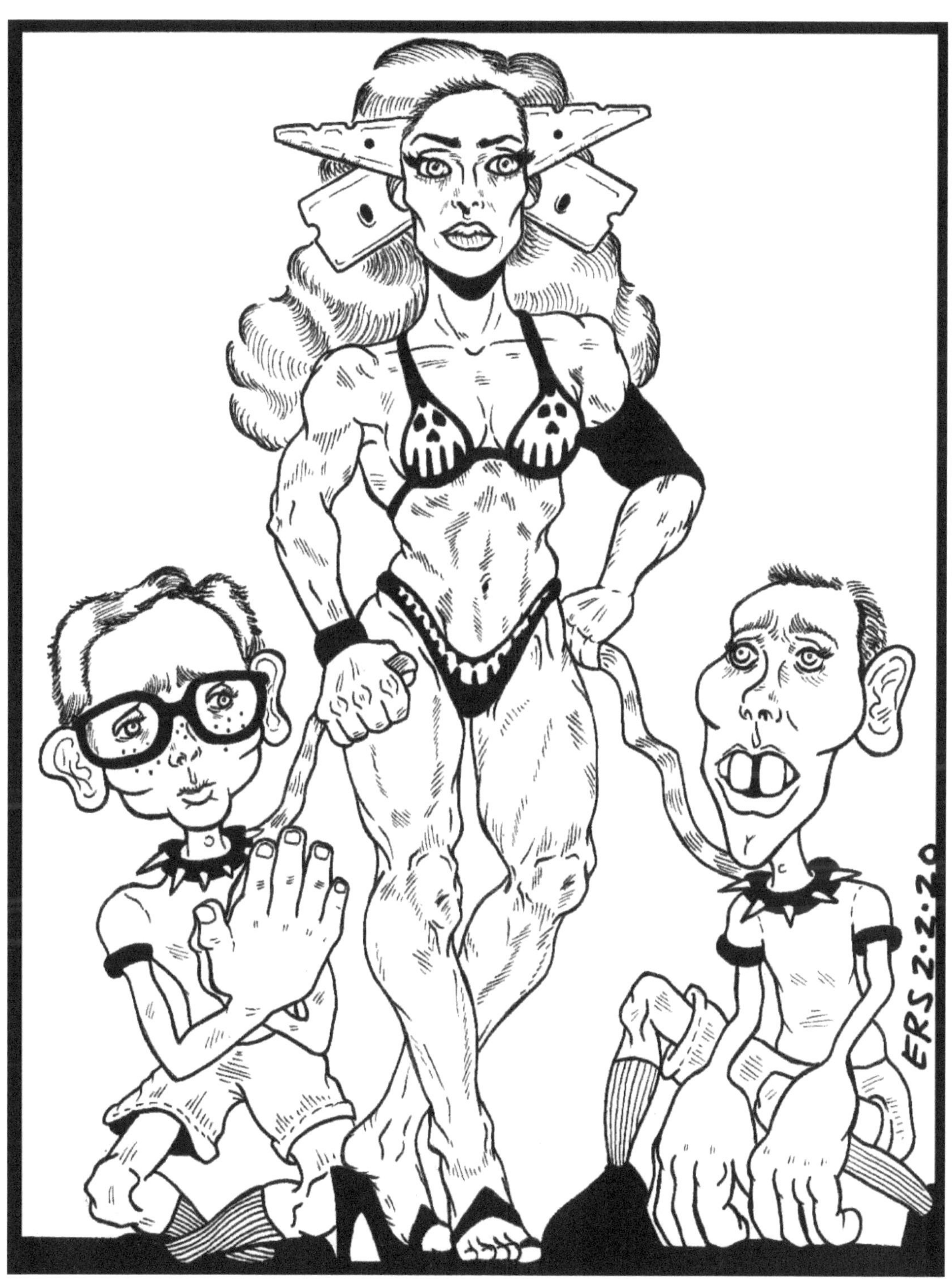

Nerd Culture Bottomed Out

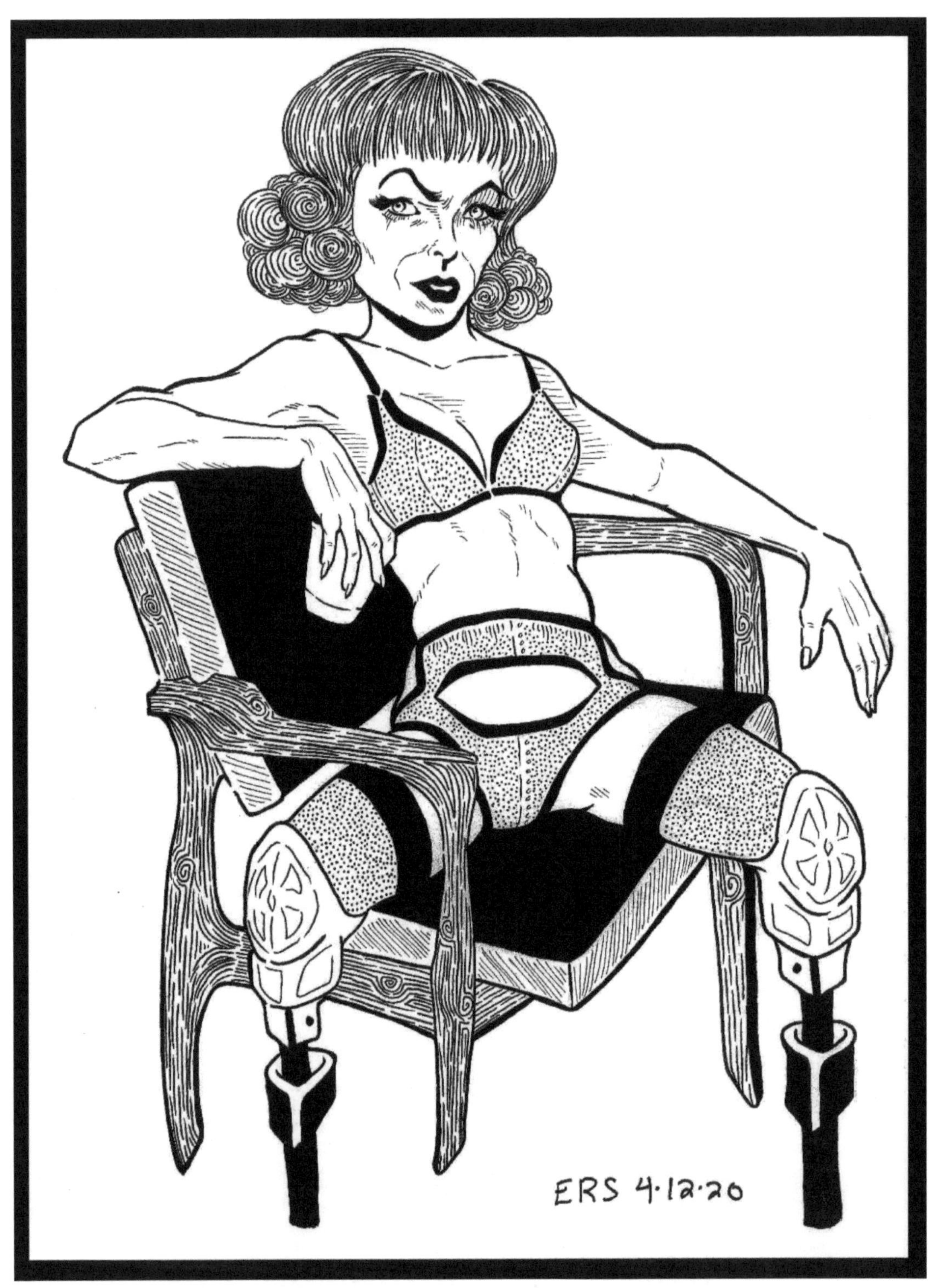

Resting Dance Partner

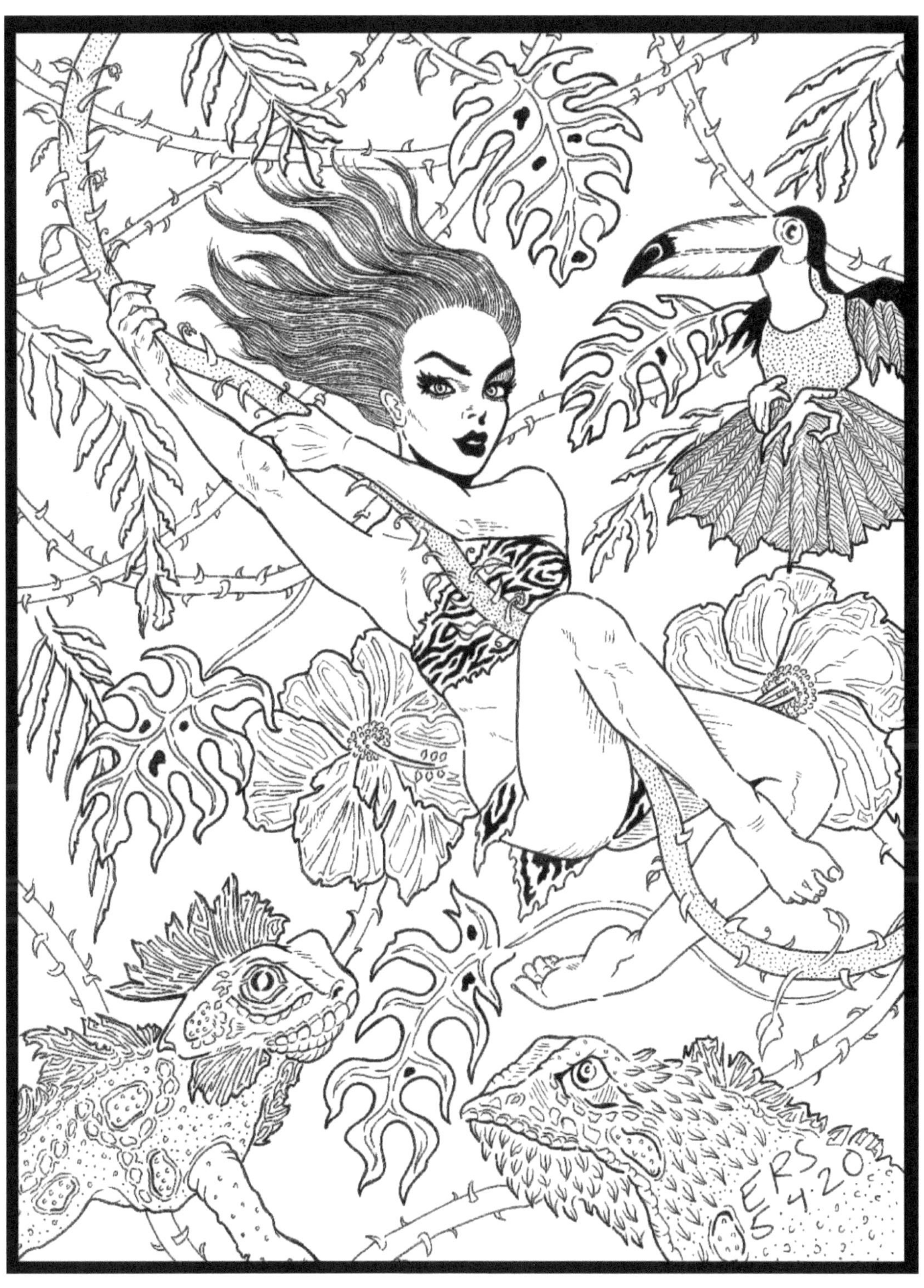

Swinger Party

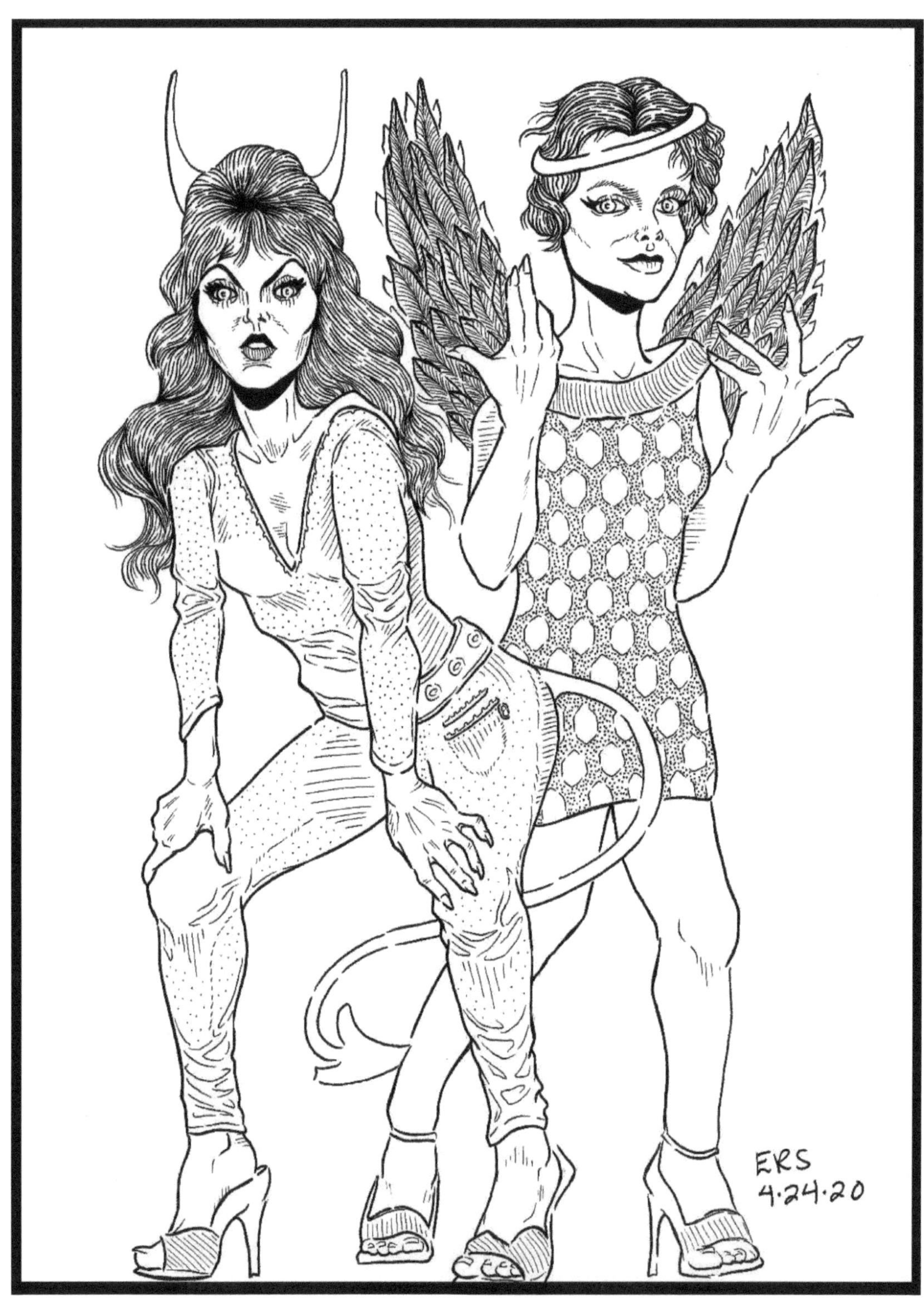

Unwelcome Stereotypes

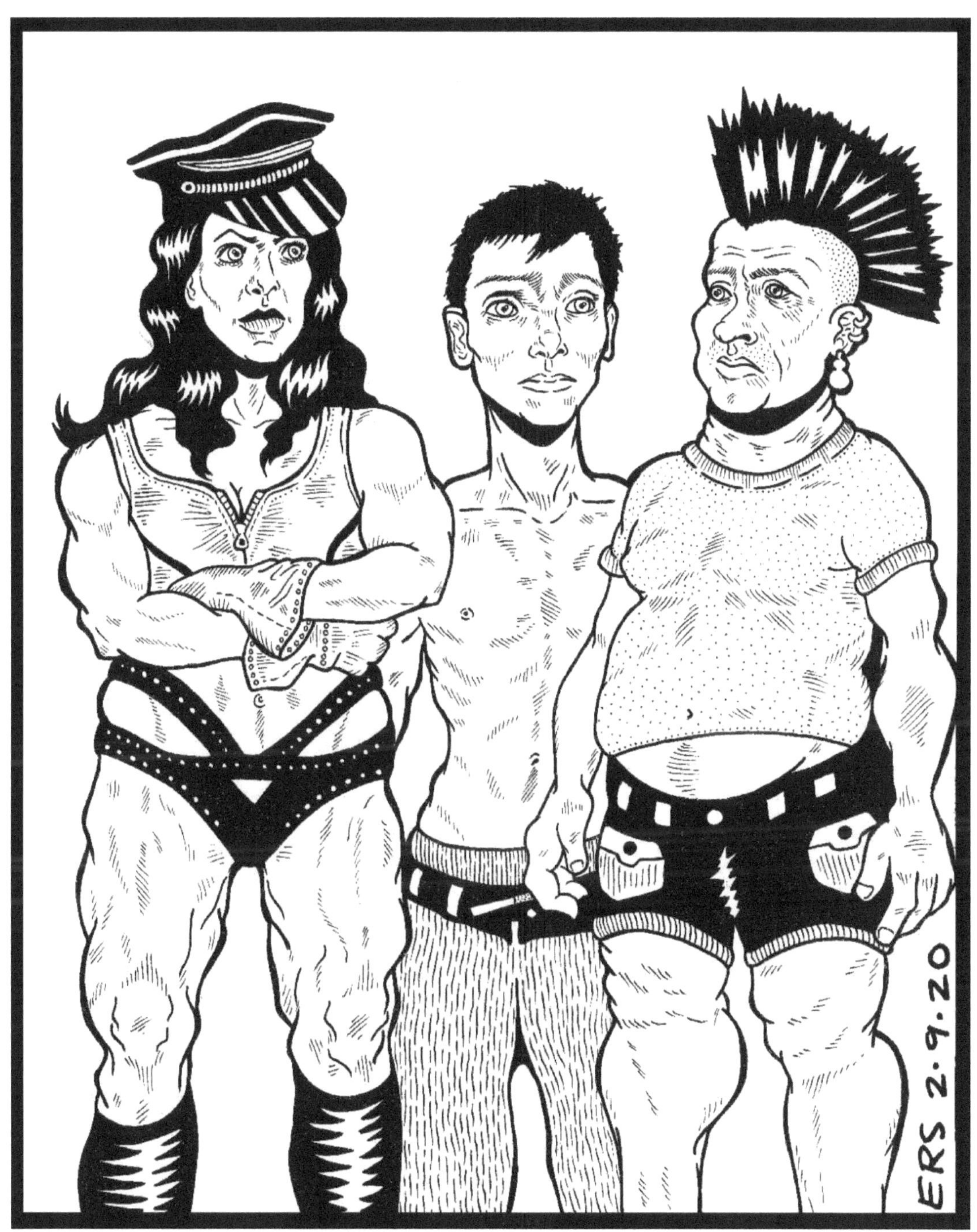

Punk Show Posse

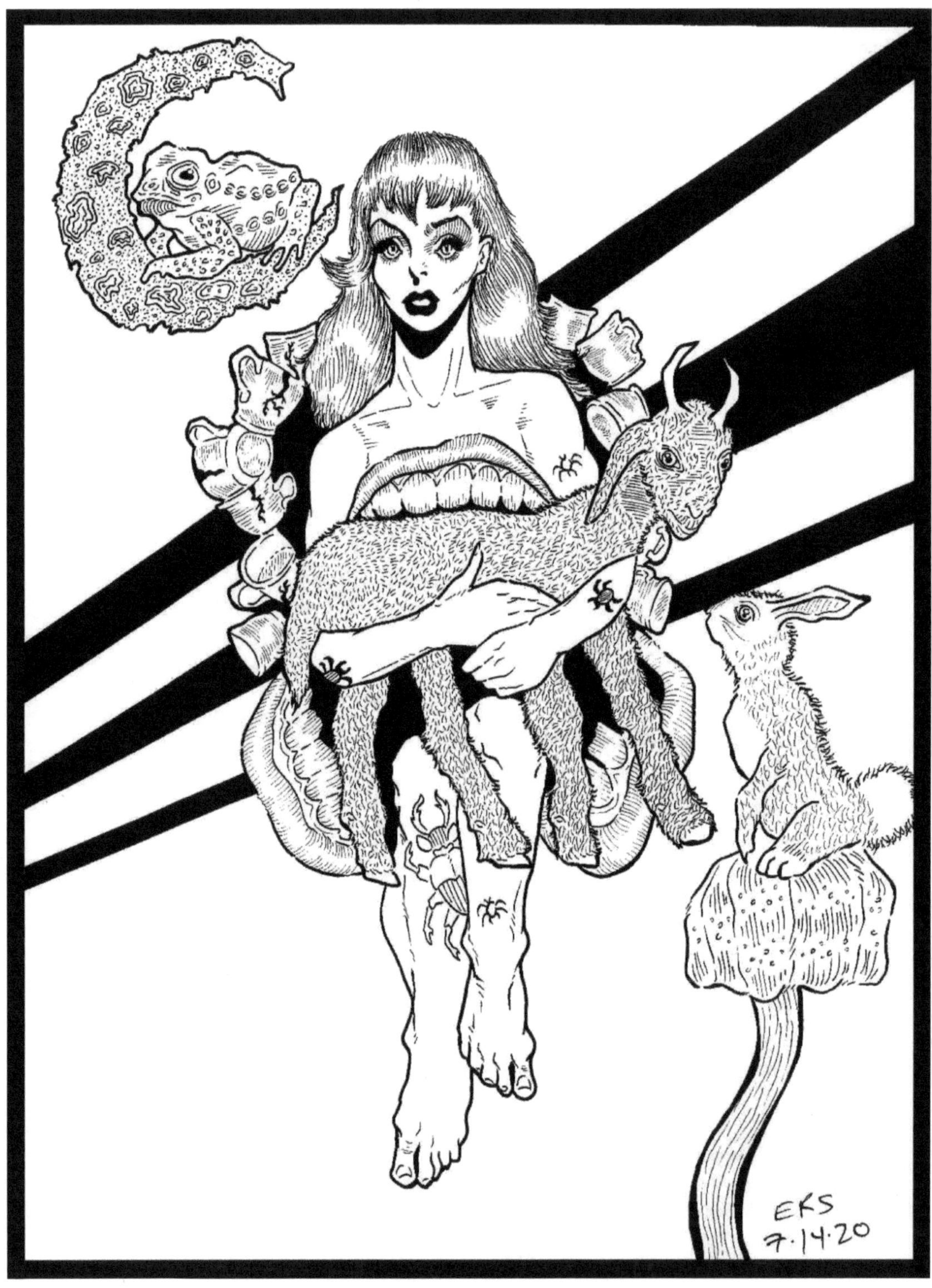

Lunar Blonde

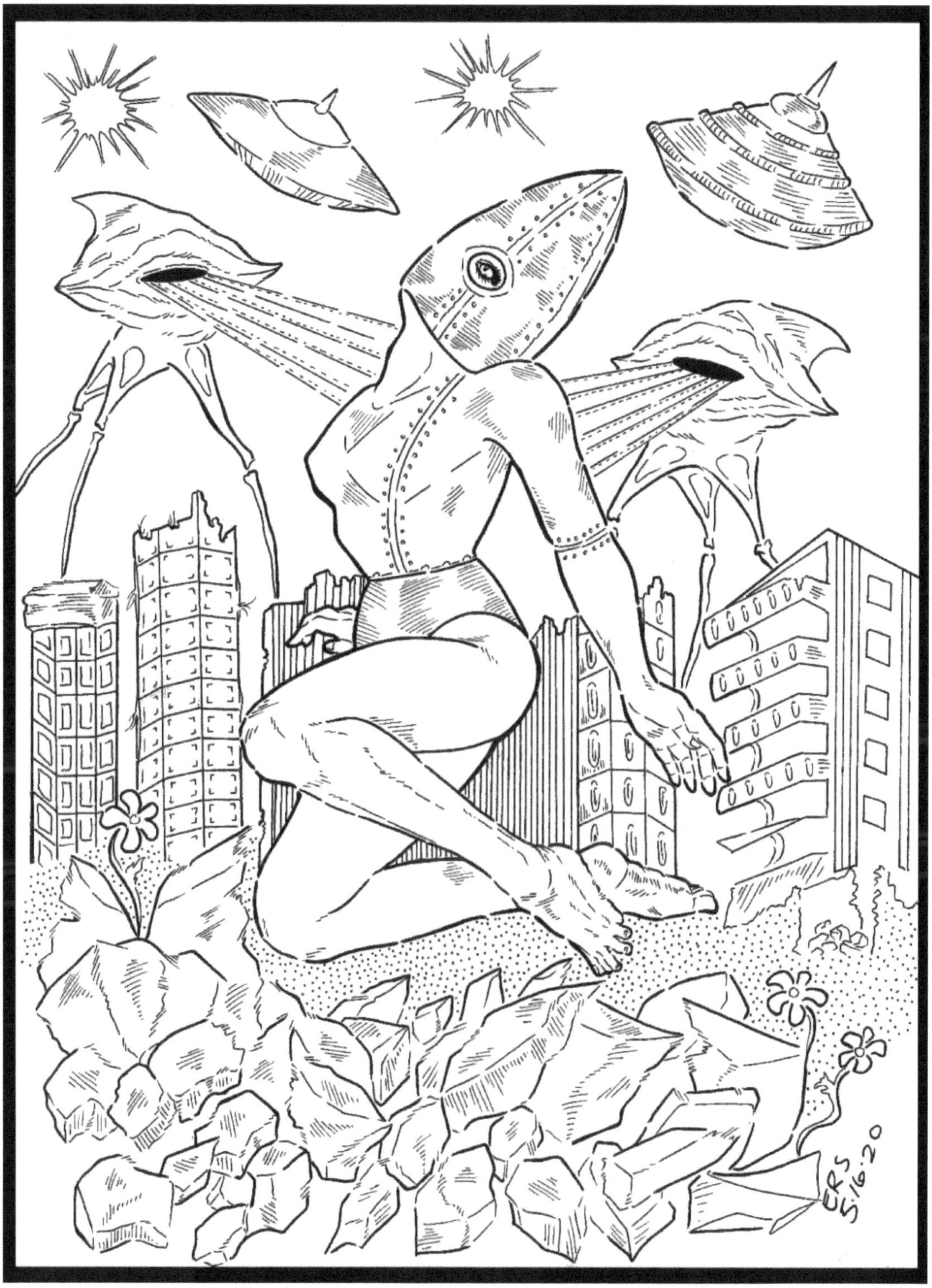

Missile Maiden Invasion

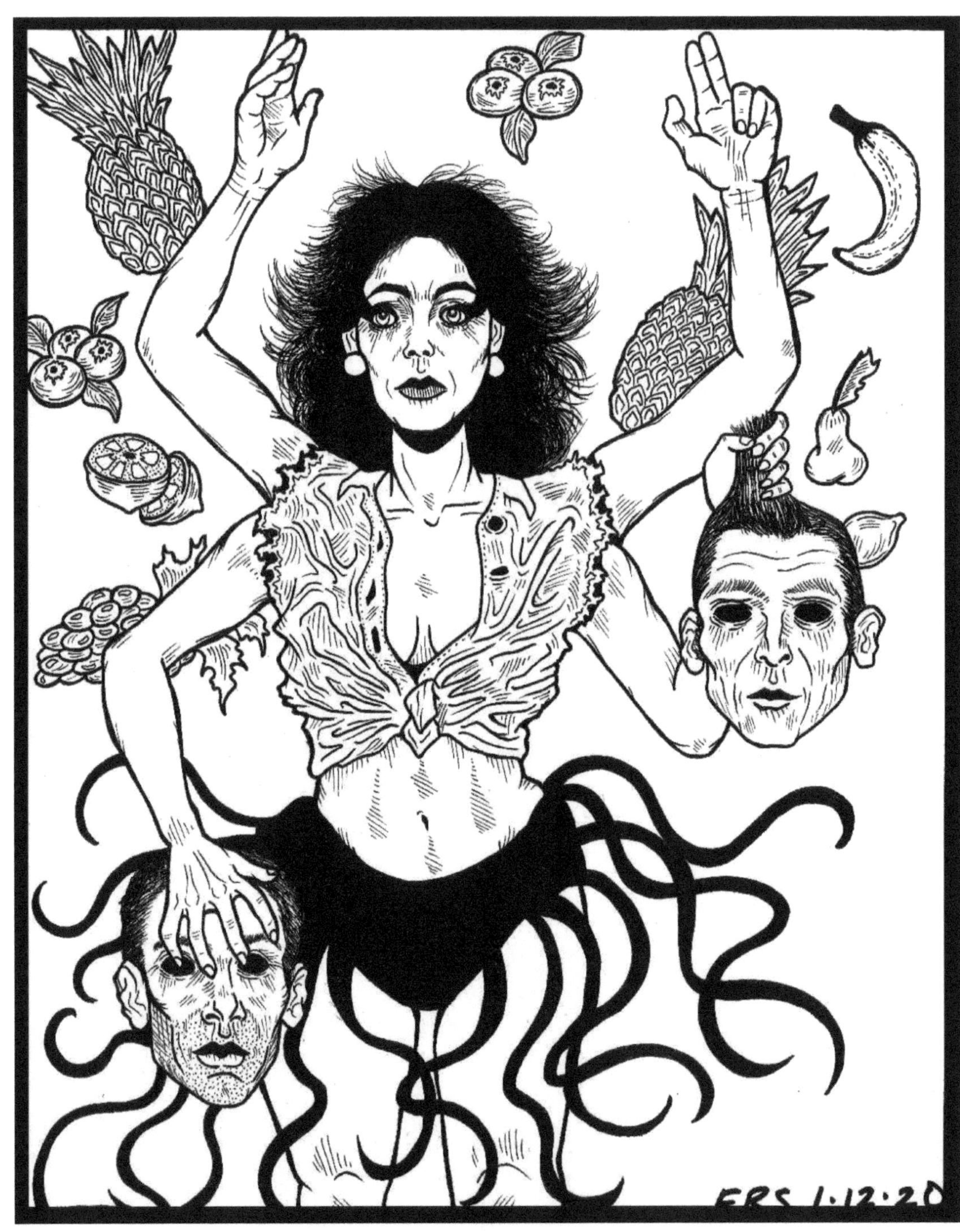

Nutrients Required

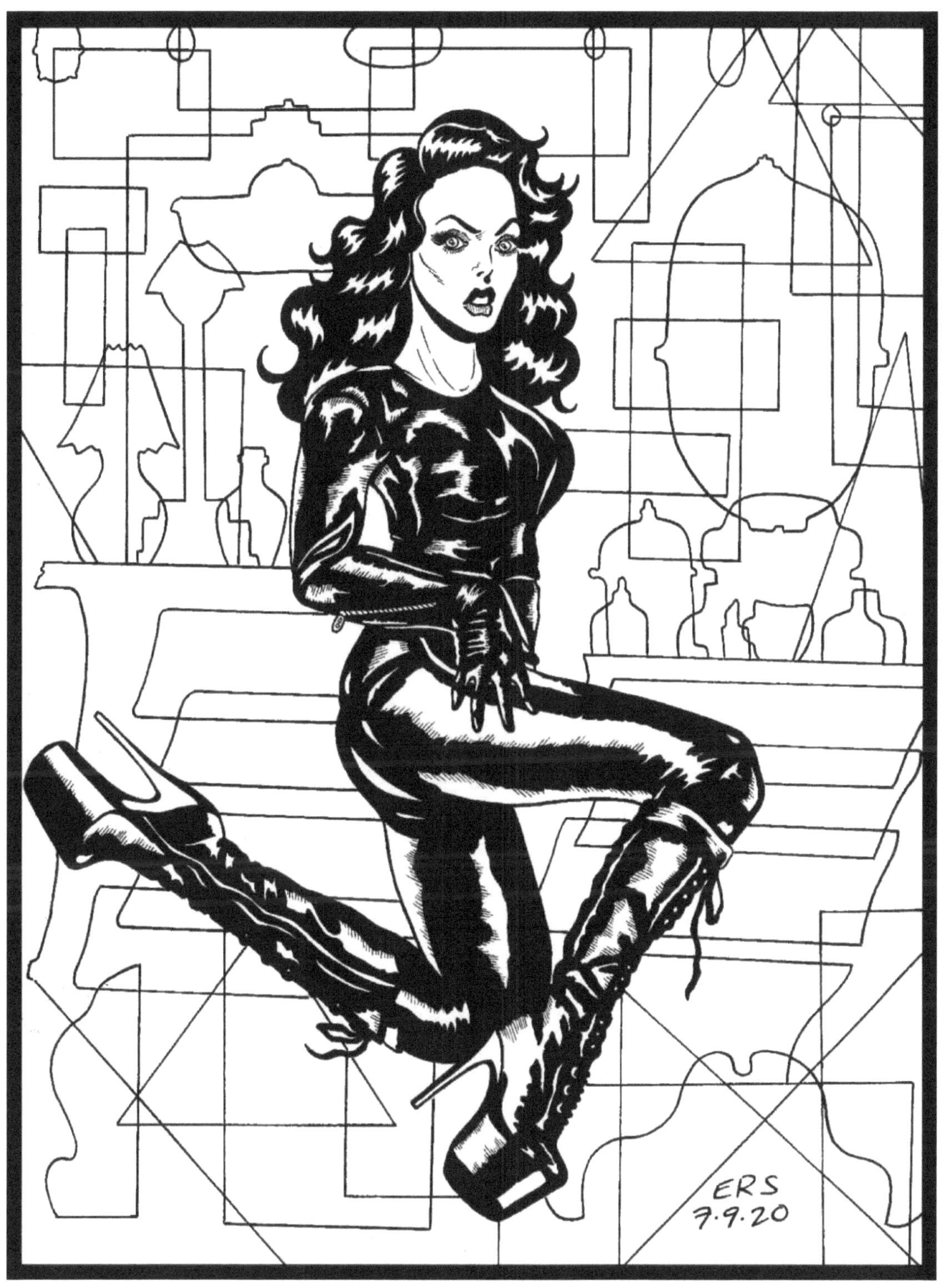

Feel the Fury

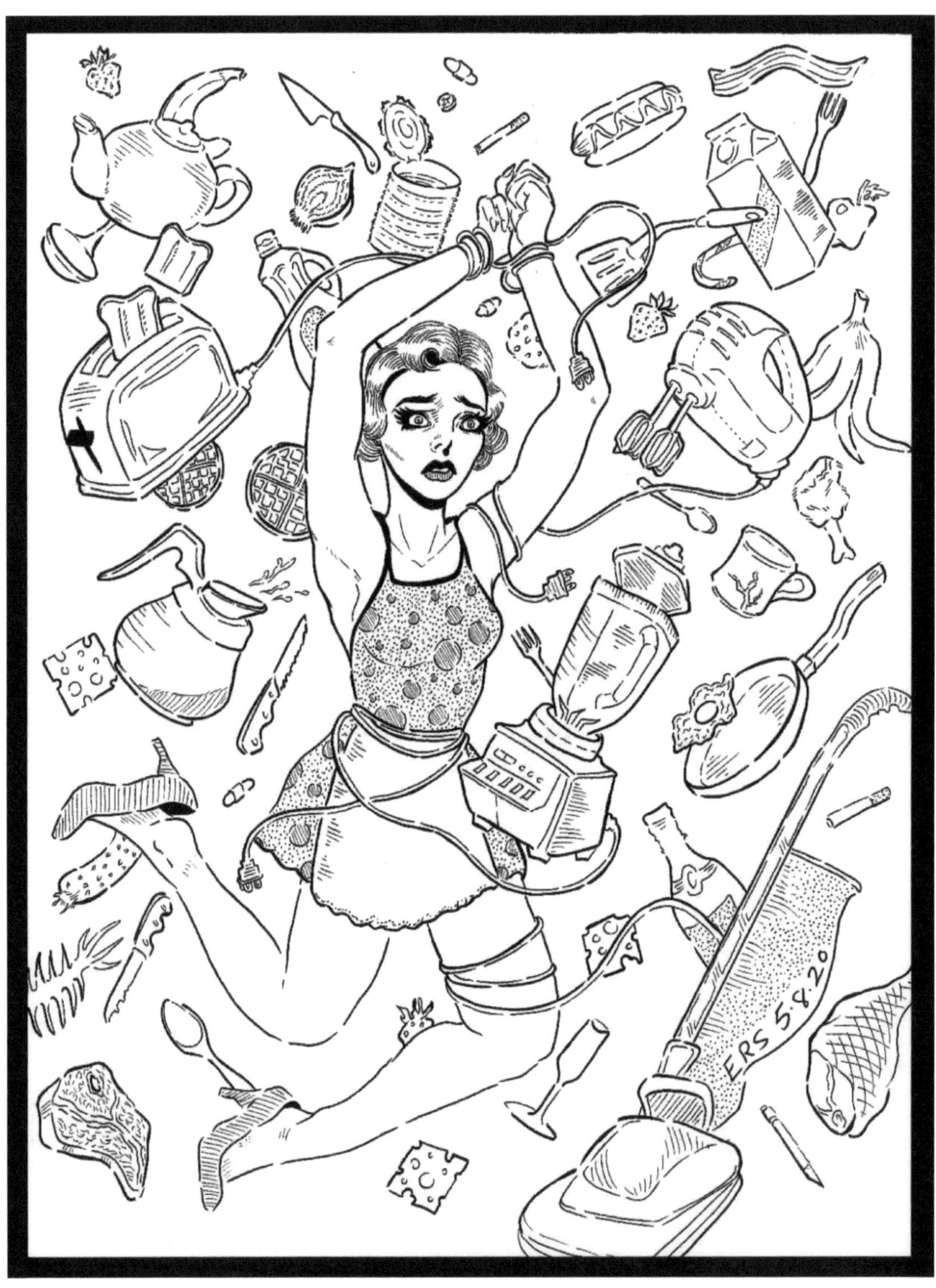

Captive Housewife

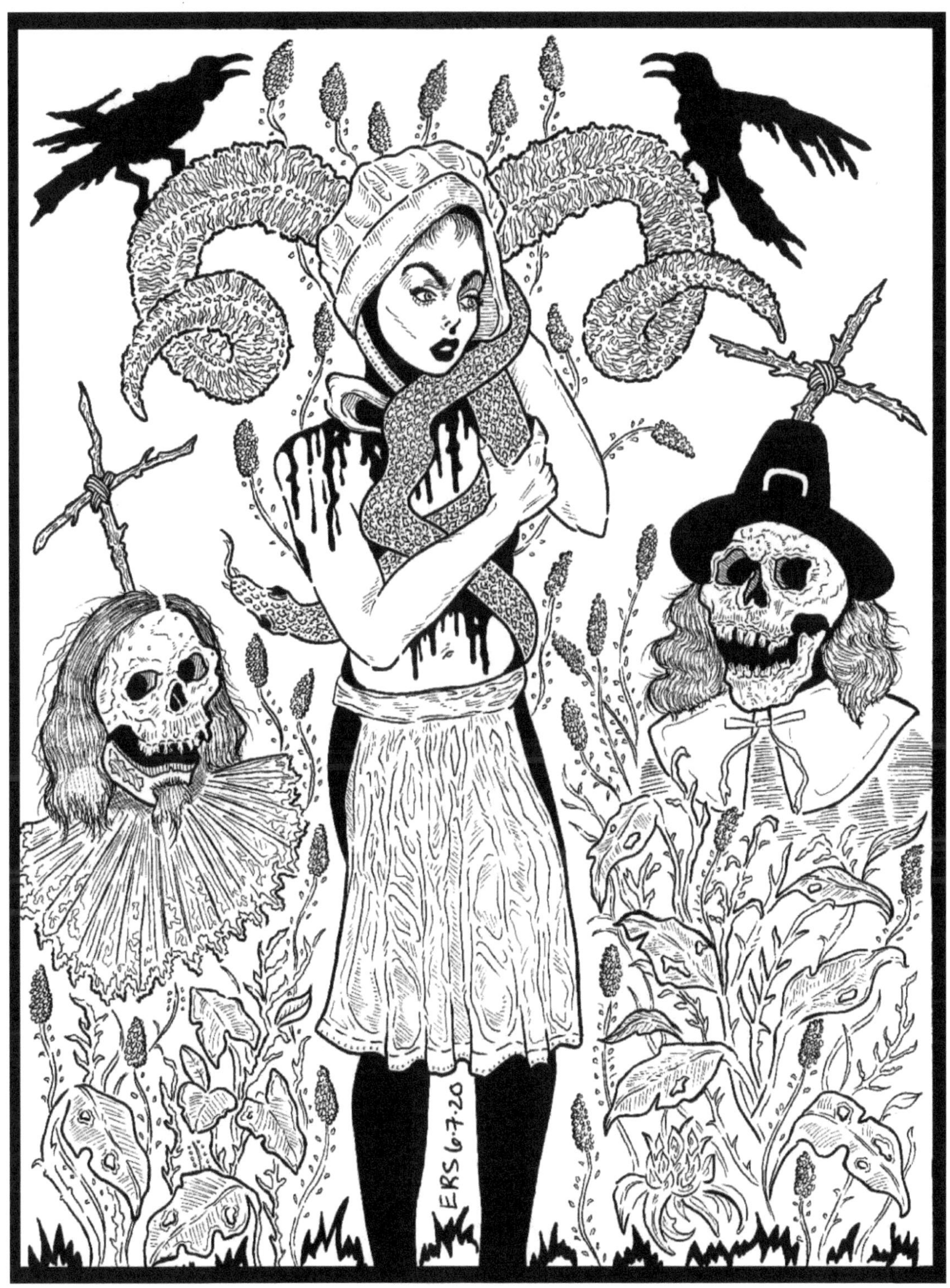

Harvesting a Goody

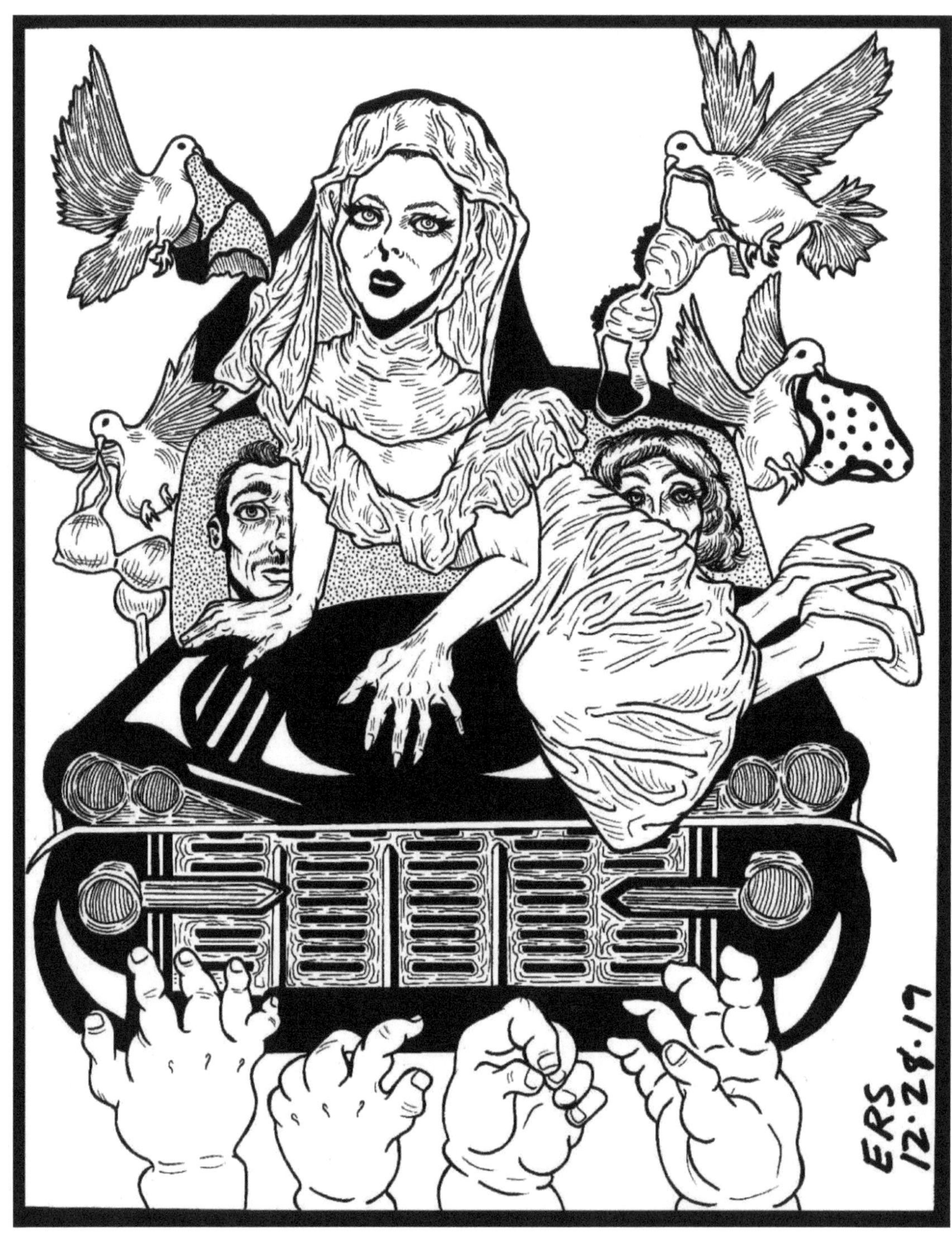

The Pro-Choice Pontiac

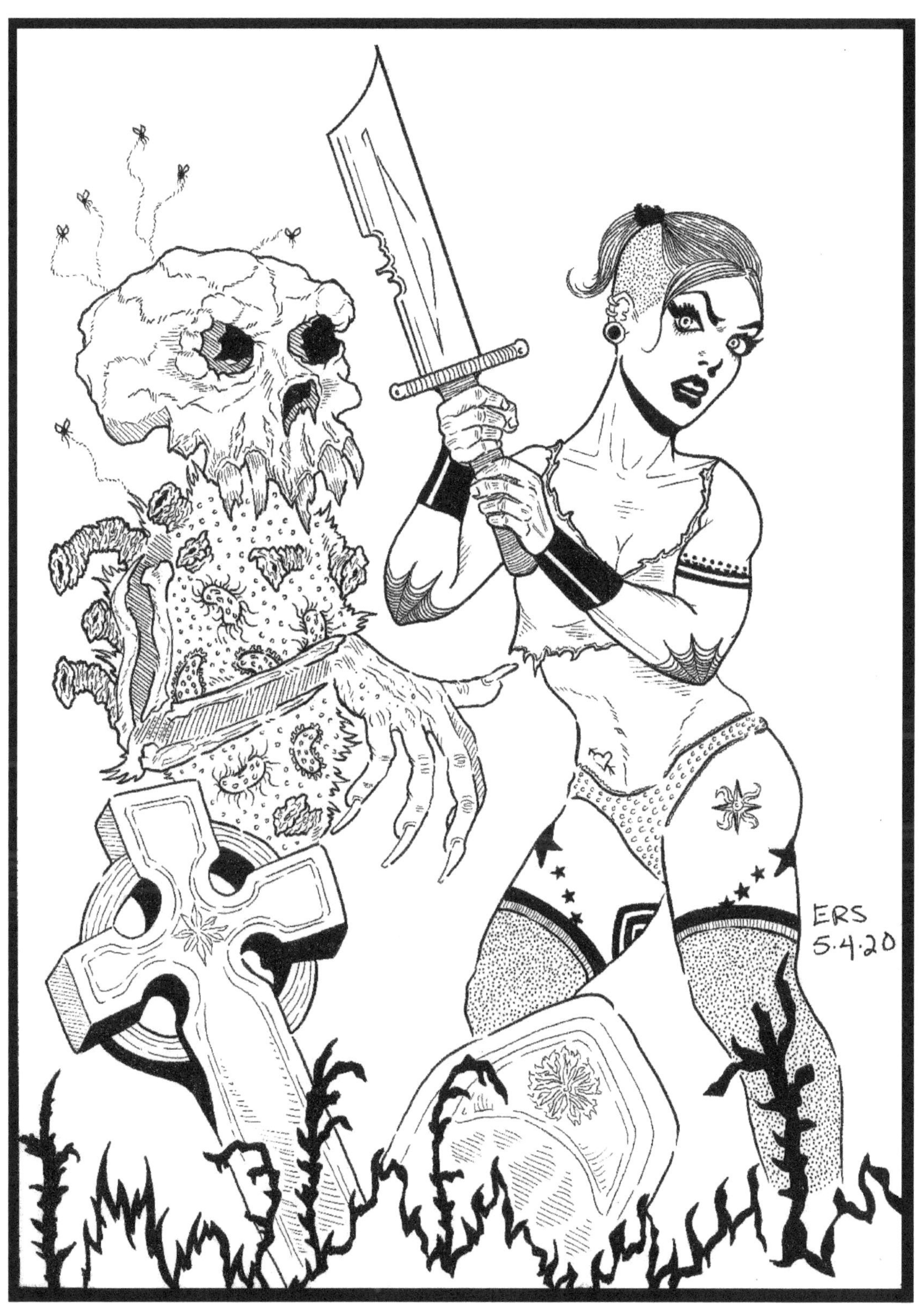

Punk v Pandemic

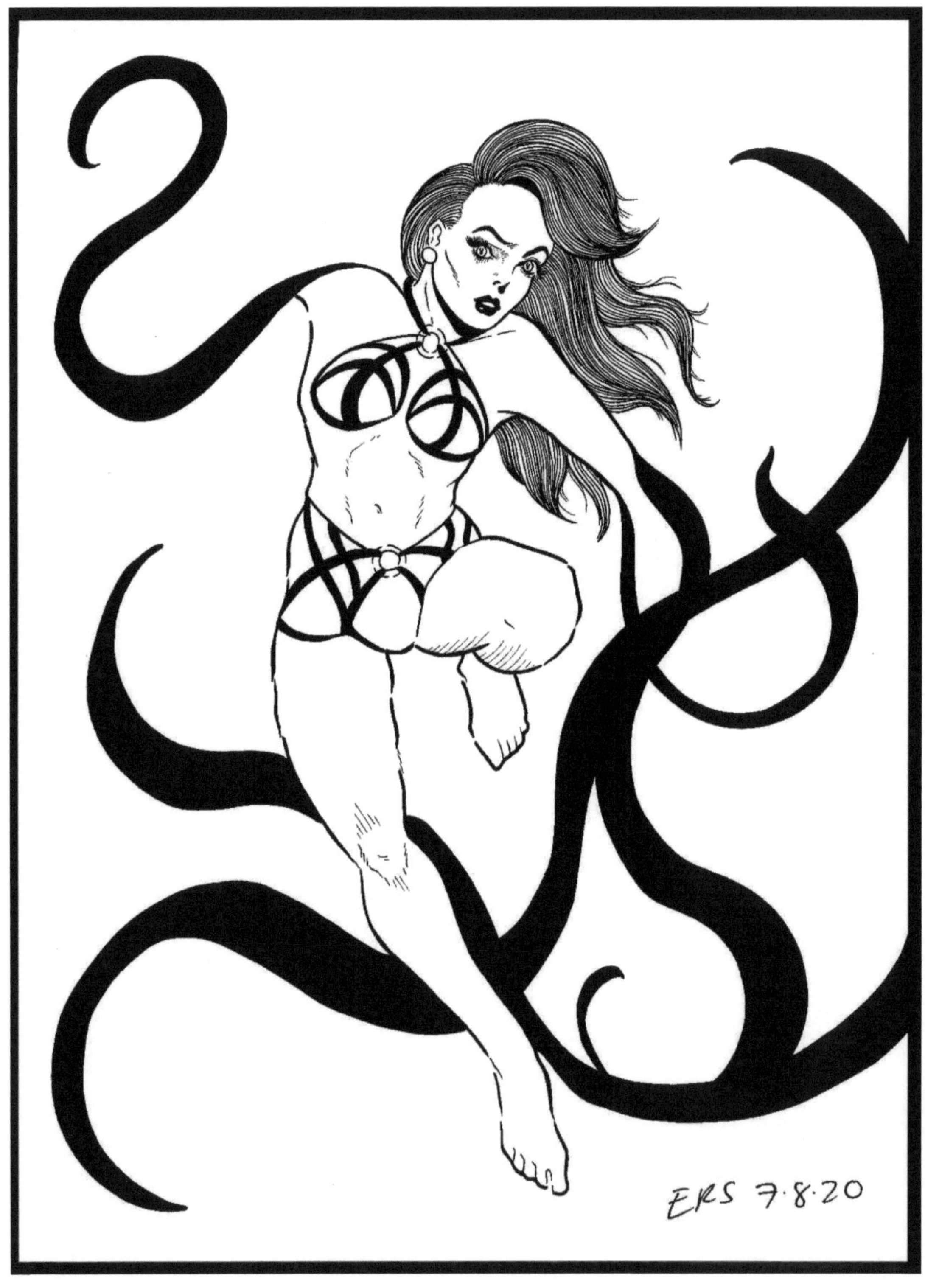

Kraken Concept

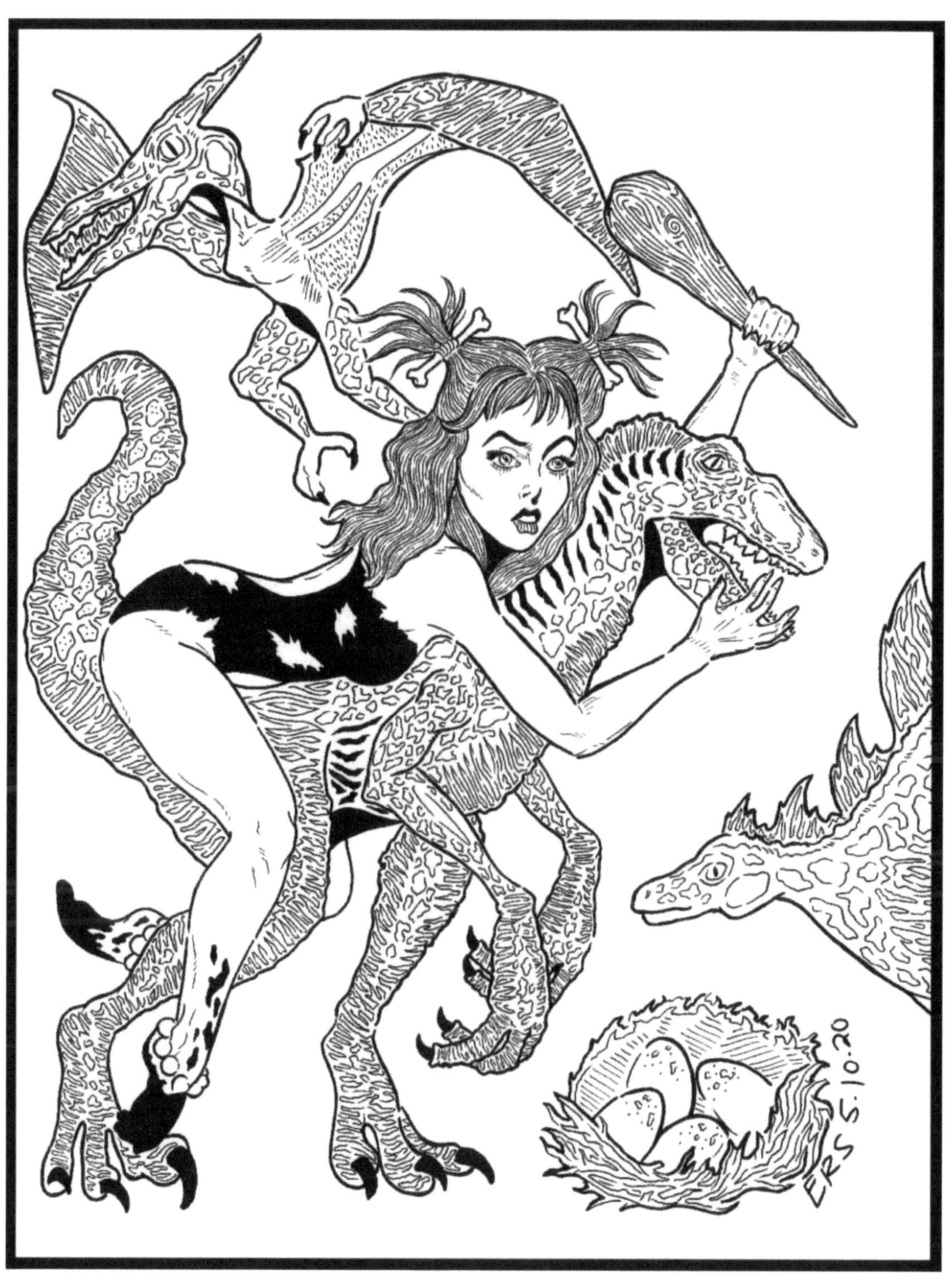

Cretaceous Queen

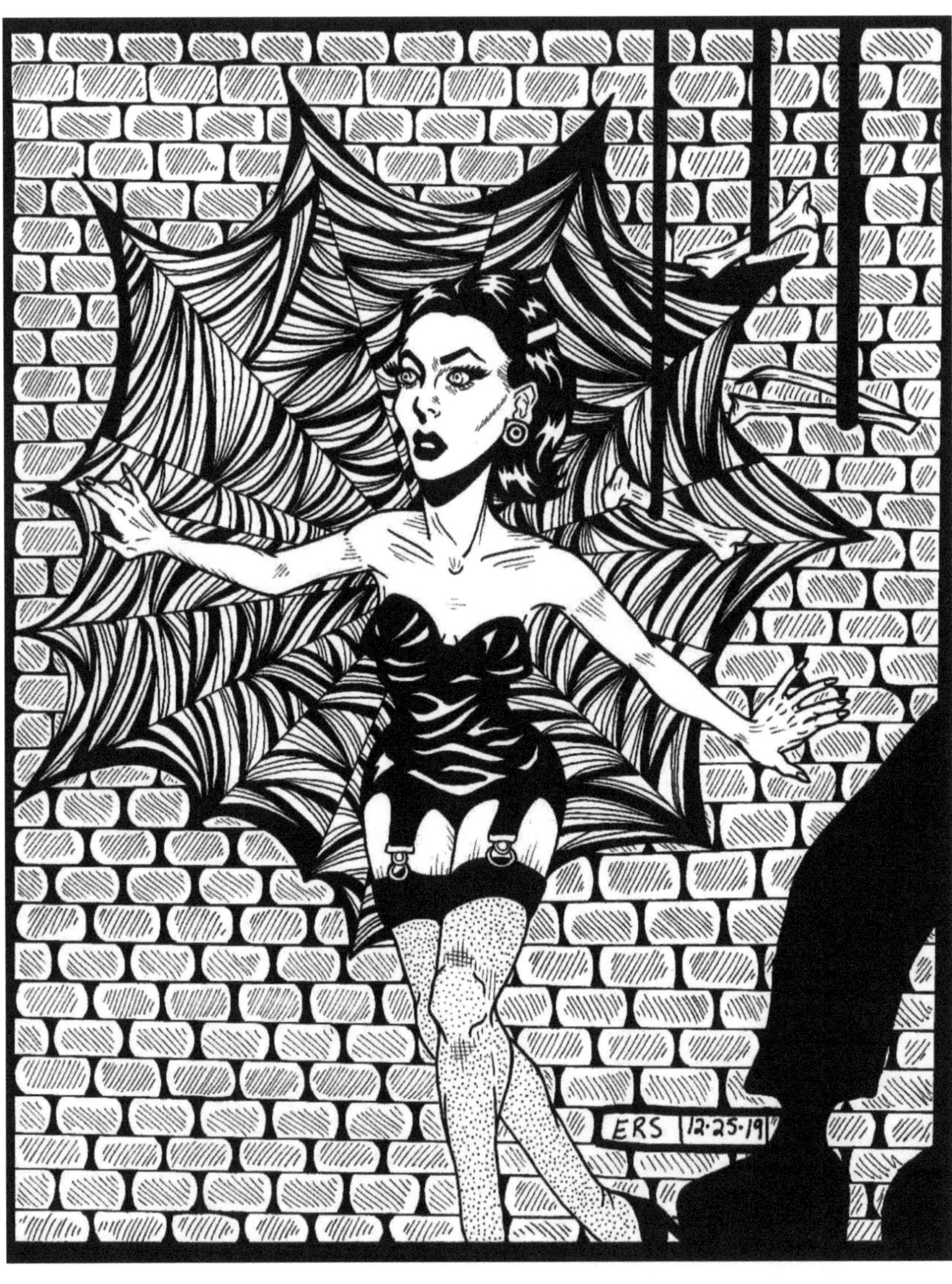

Alley Damsel

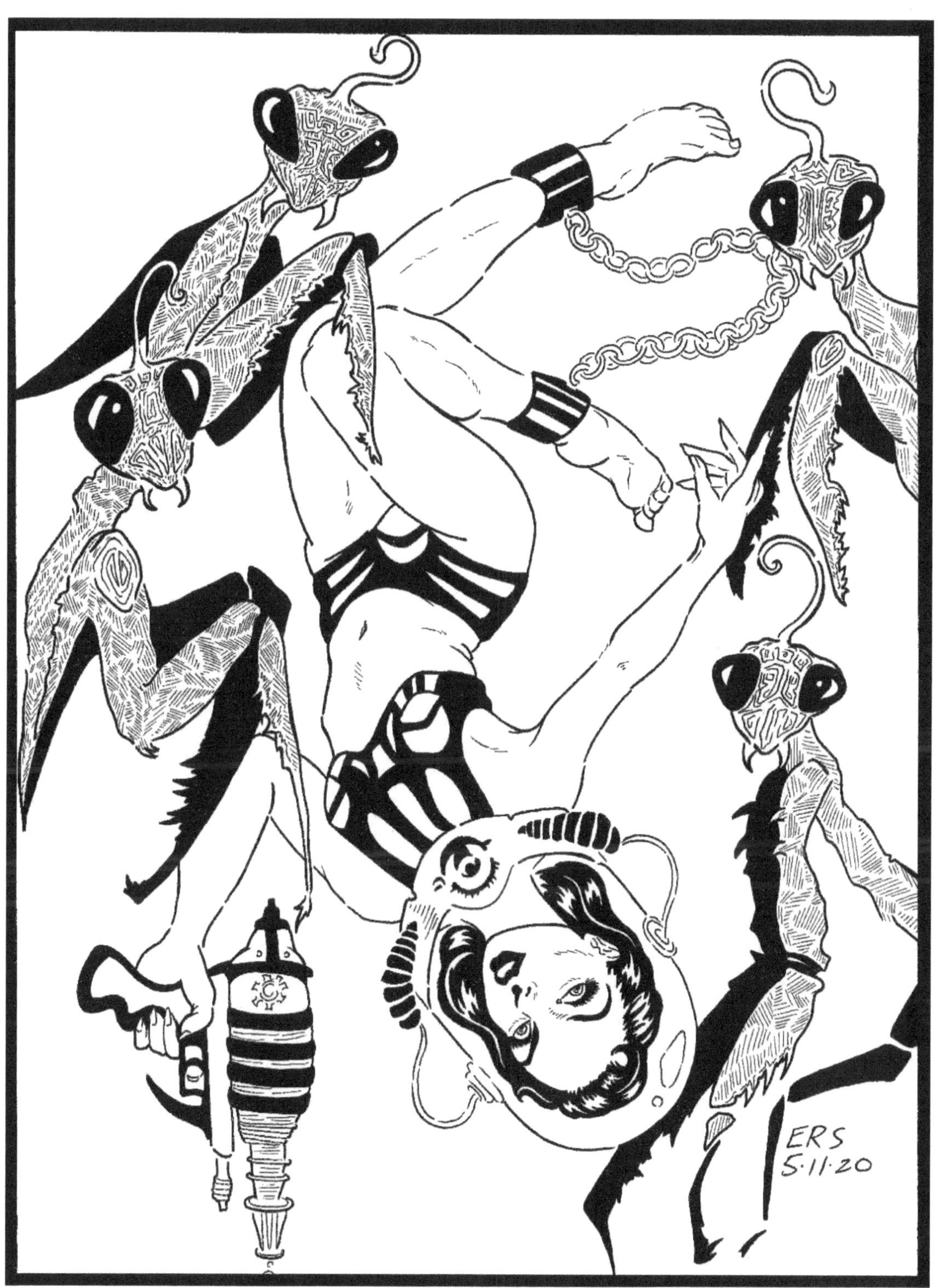

Interspecies Intergalactic Gang Bang

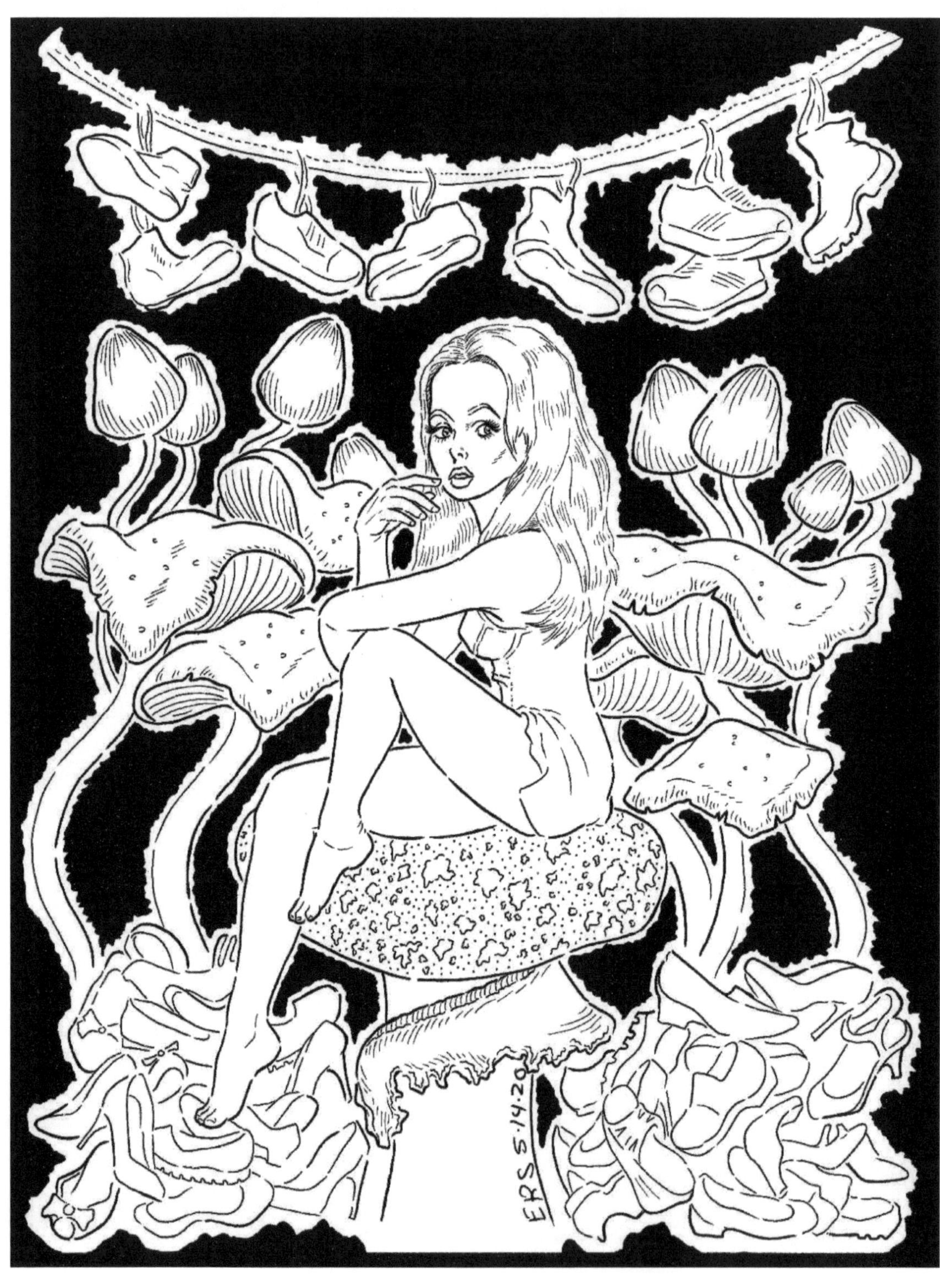

Cannibal Nymph

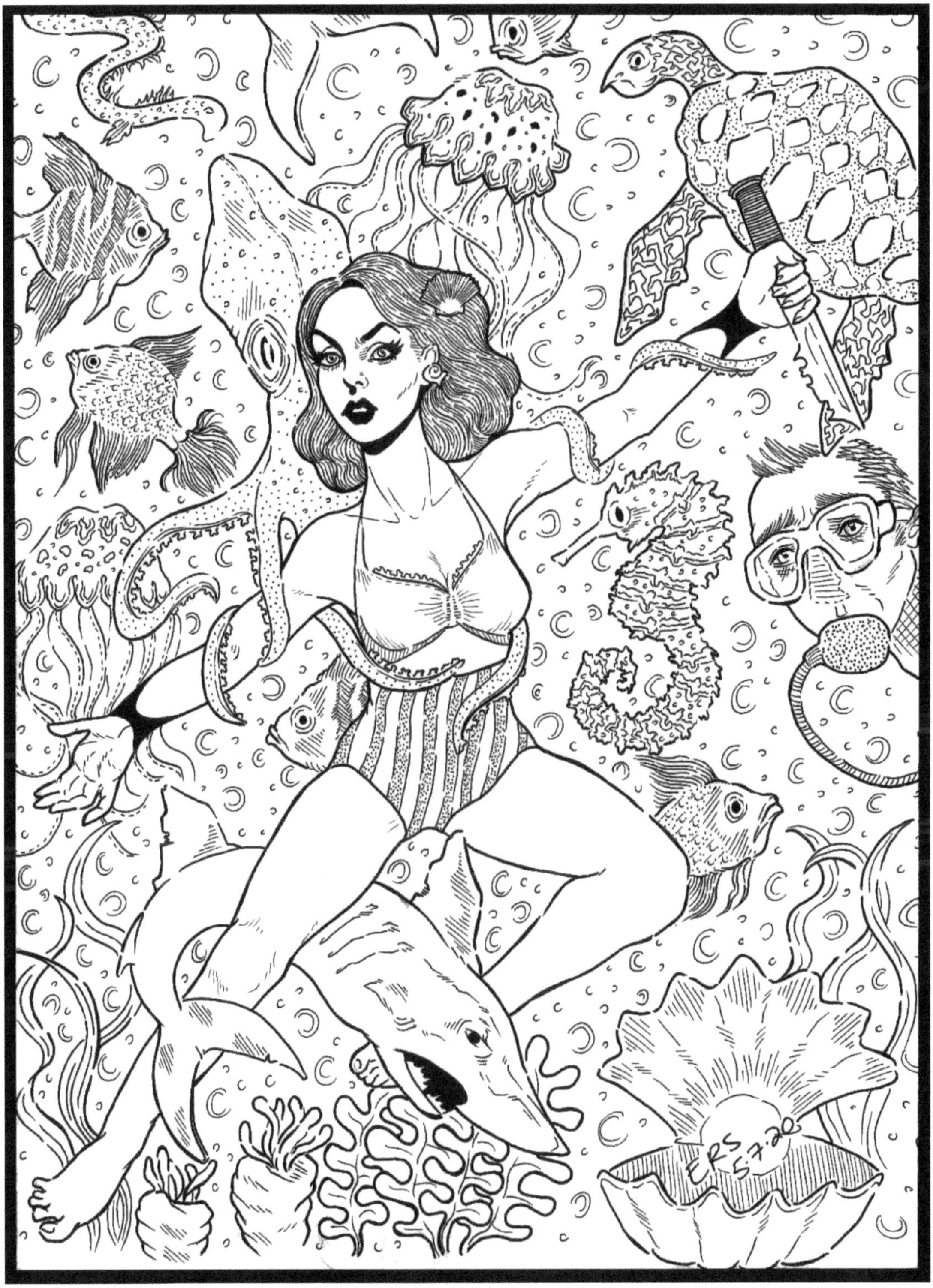

Underwater Warrior

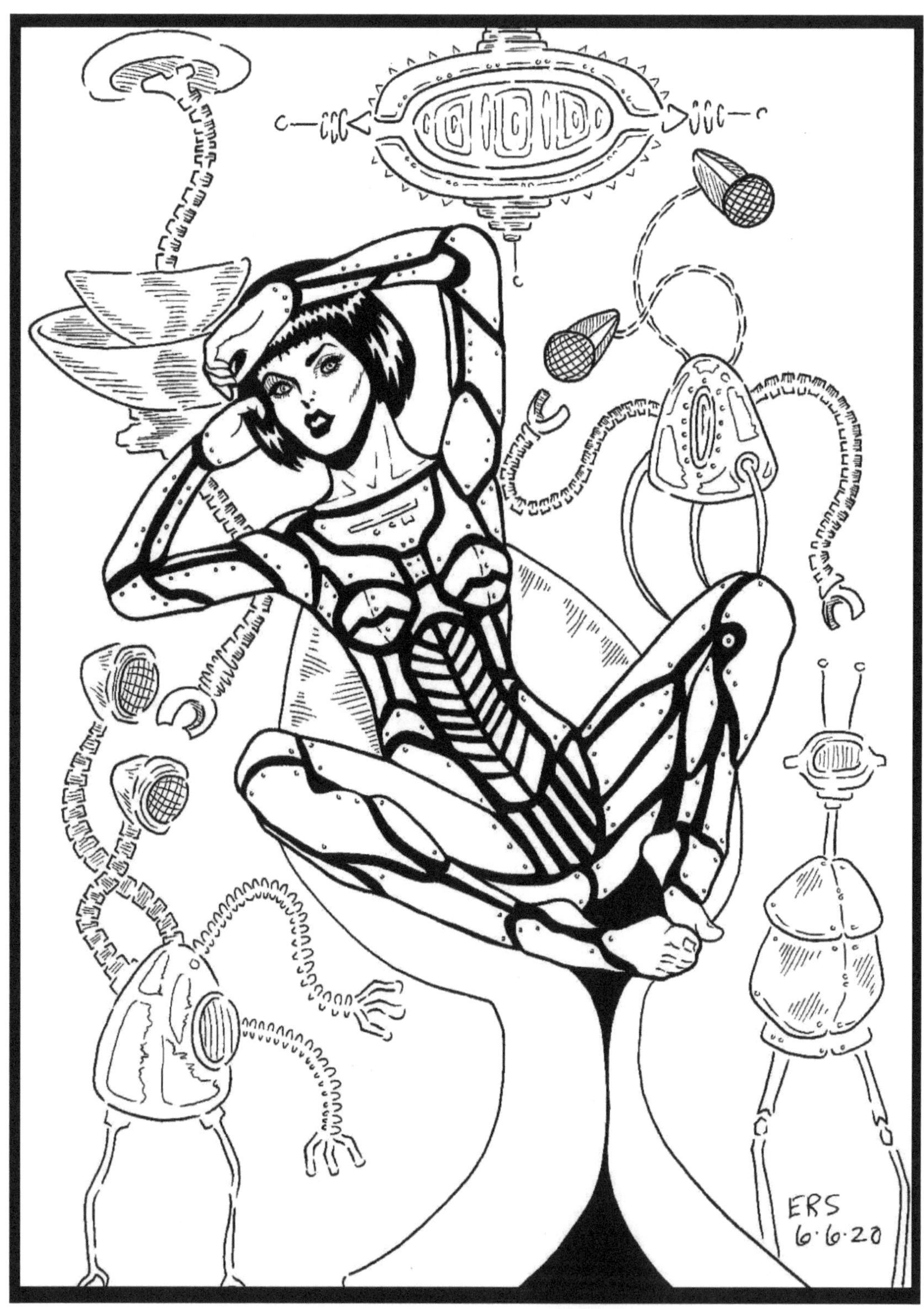

Living Room Servants

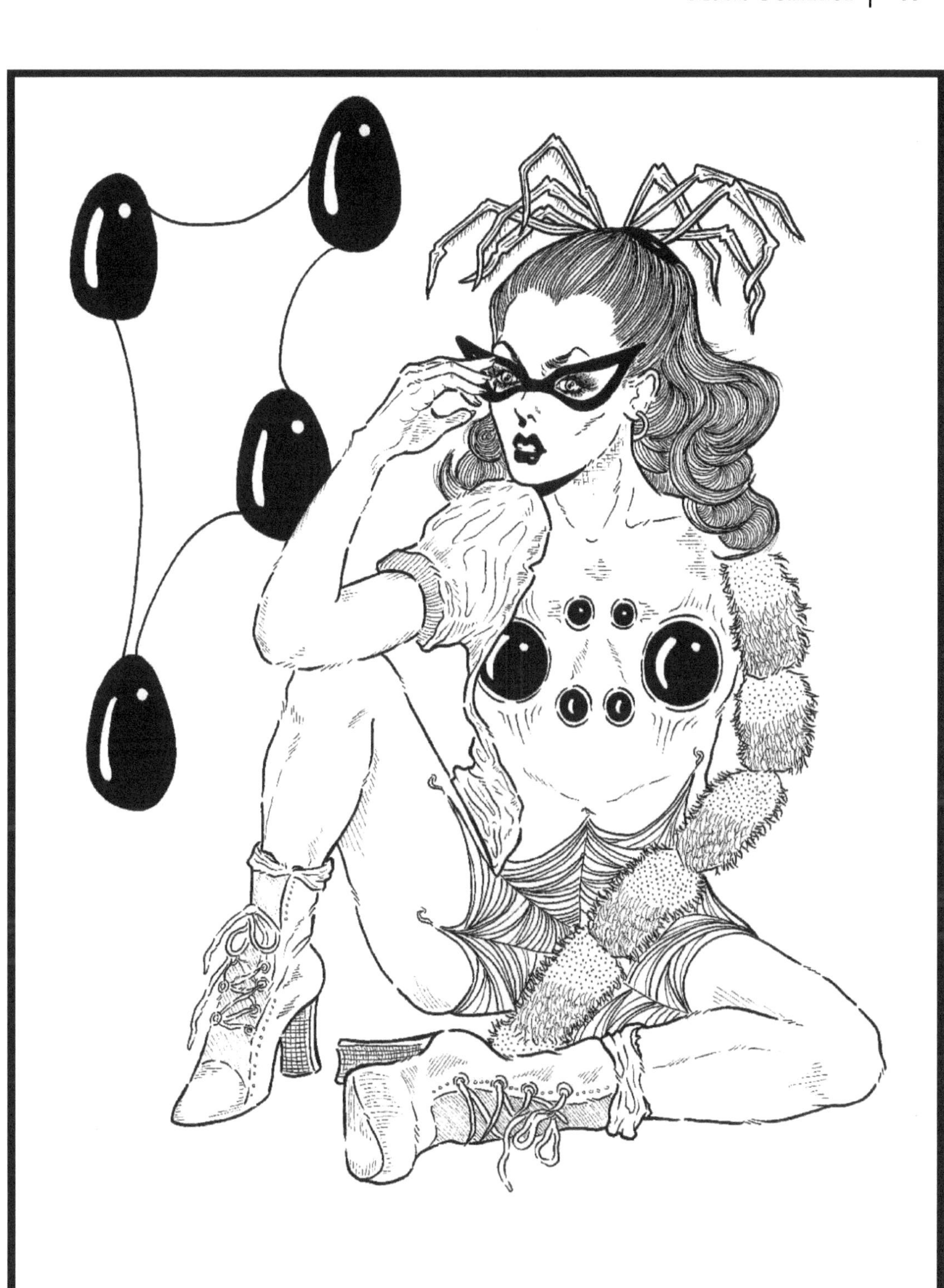

Spider Heroine

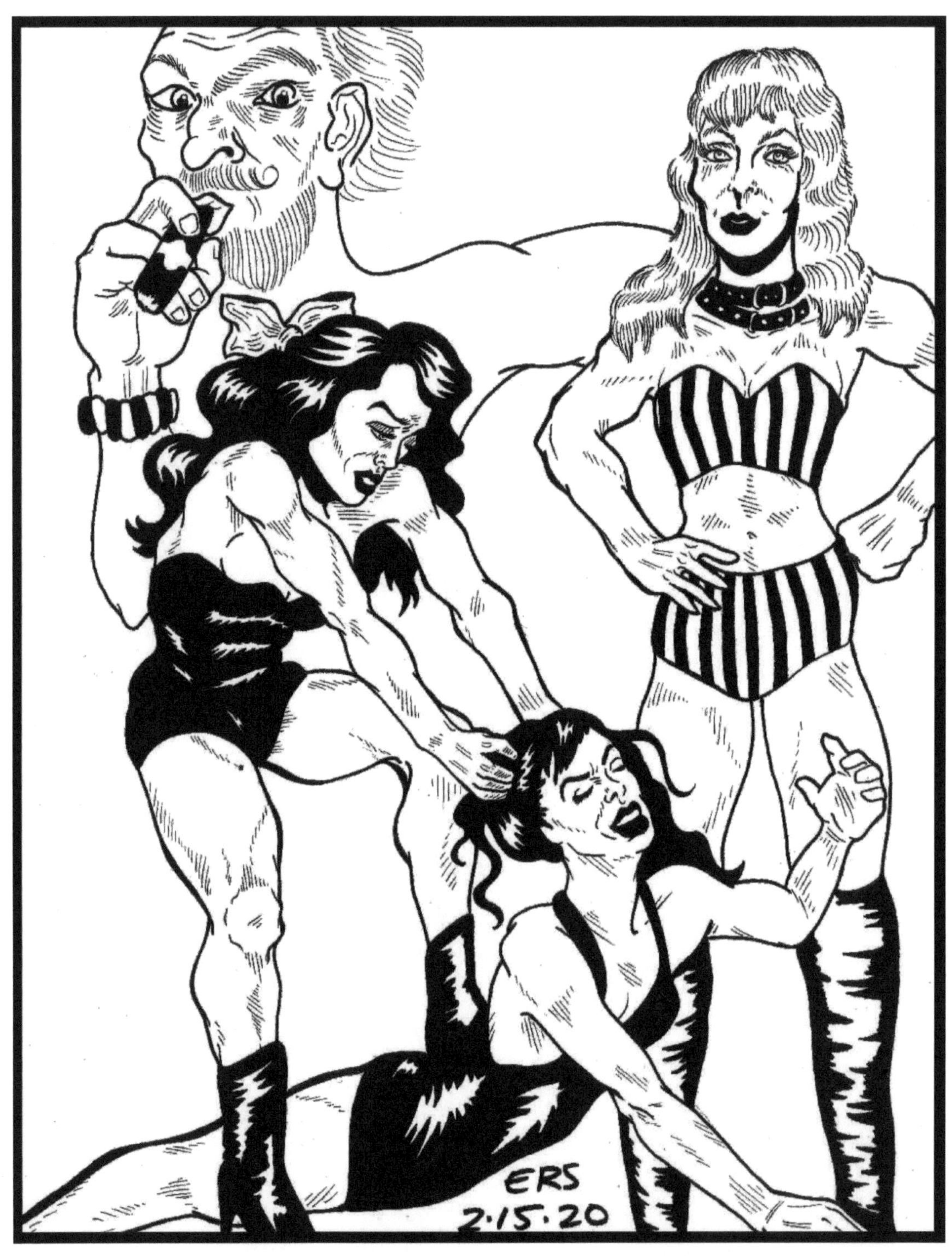

Battle for the Bow Tie

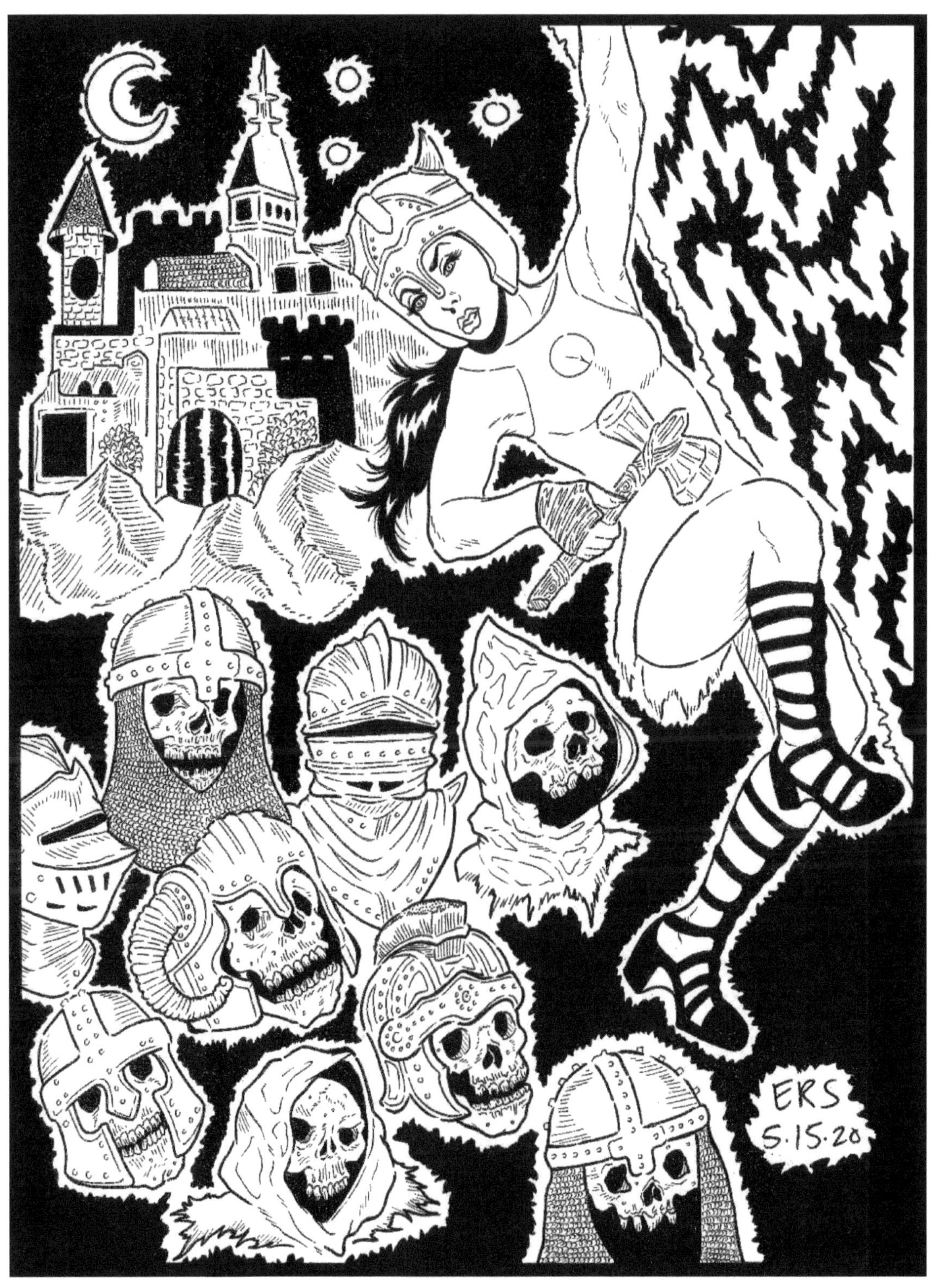

Hungry Undead Legions Unite

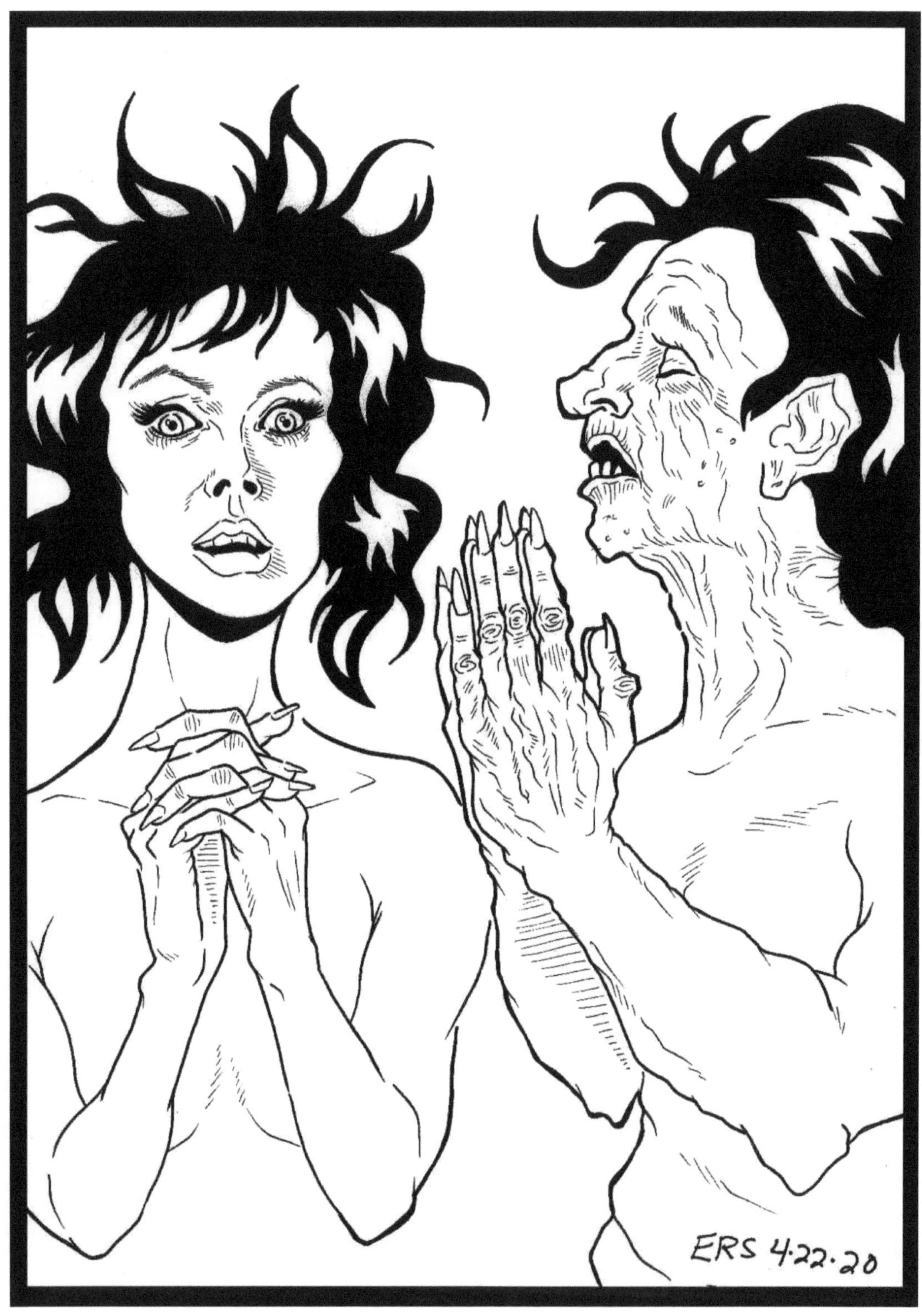

Prayer for Eternal Youth

III. Lonesome Figures

Abstract: Chapter Three

Ensuing visages focus on characters in isolation, singular studies of the solitary and longing. Imperial and individual, they answer only to themselves and their complex internal lives. Satirical or sincere, discrete and distinct, each is undeniably themselves, whether they like it or not.

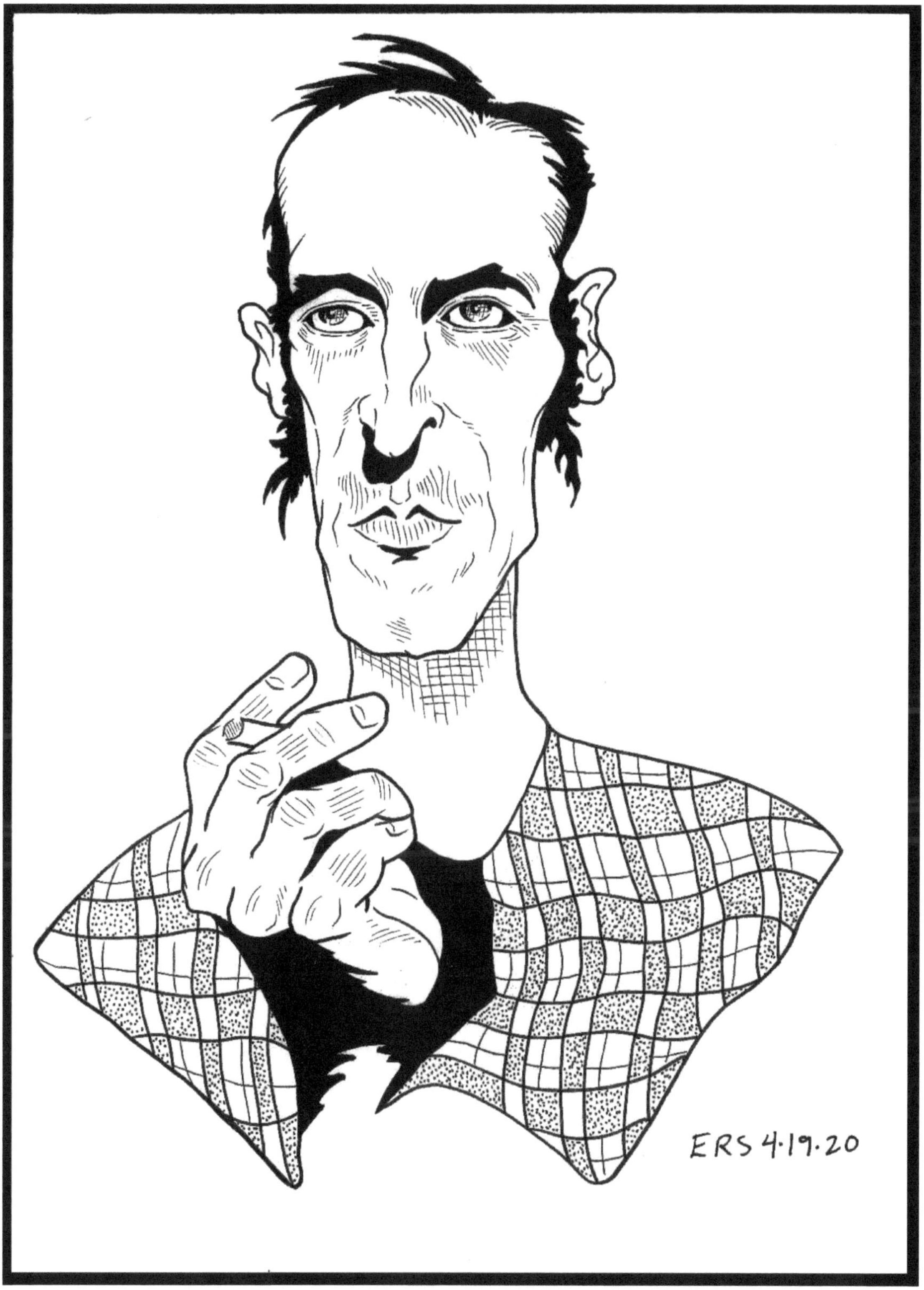

Smug Elegance

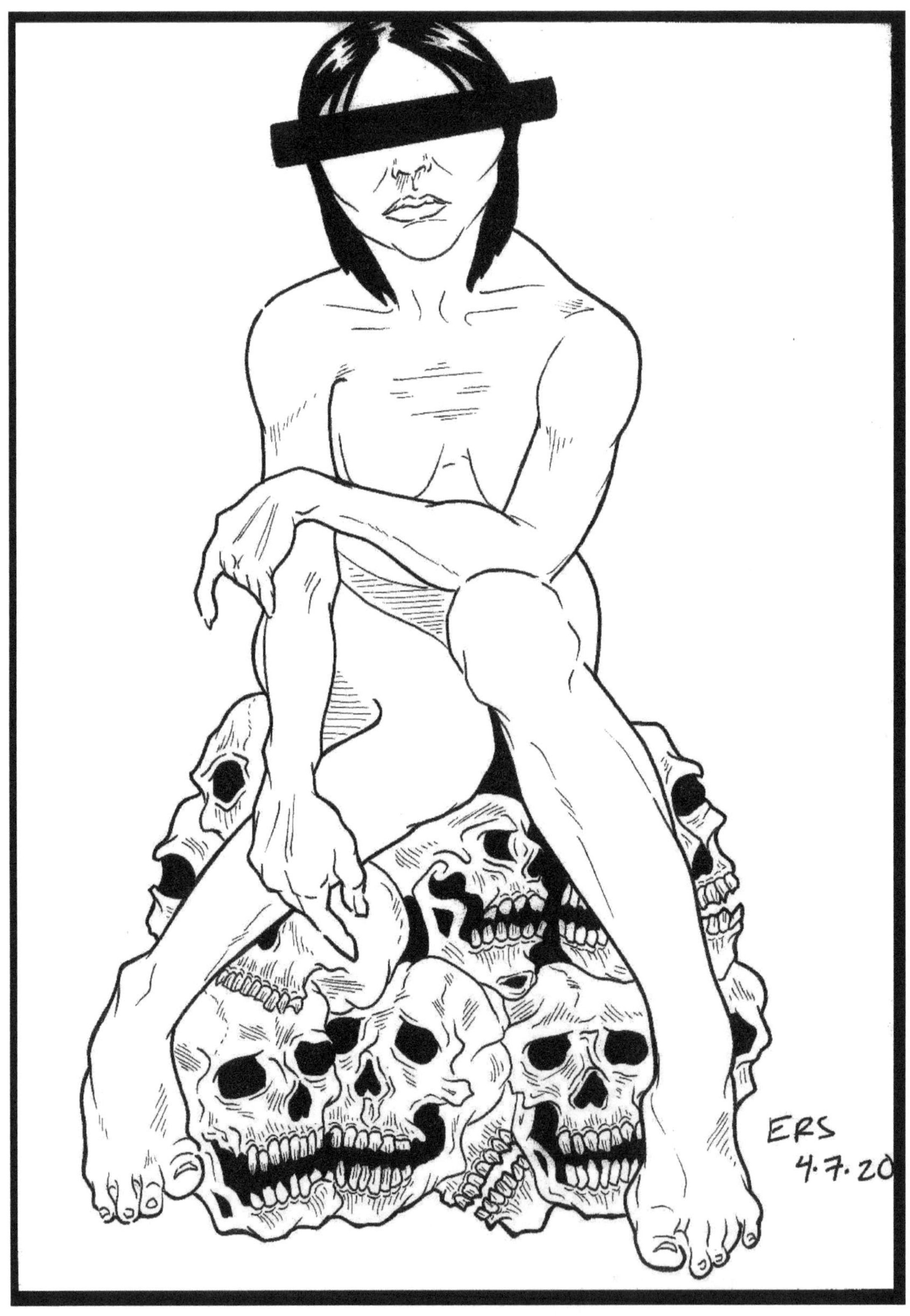

Patient Zero

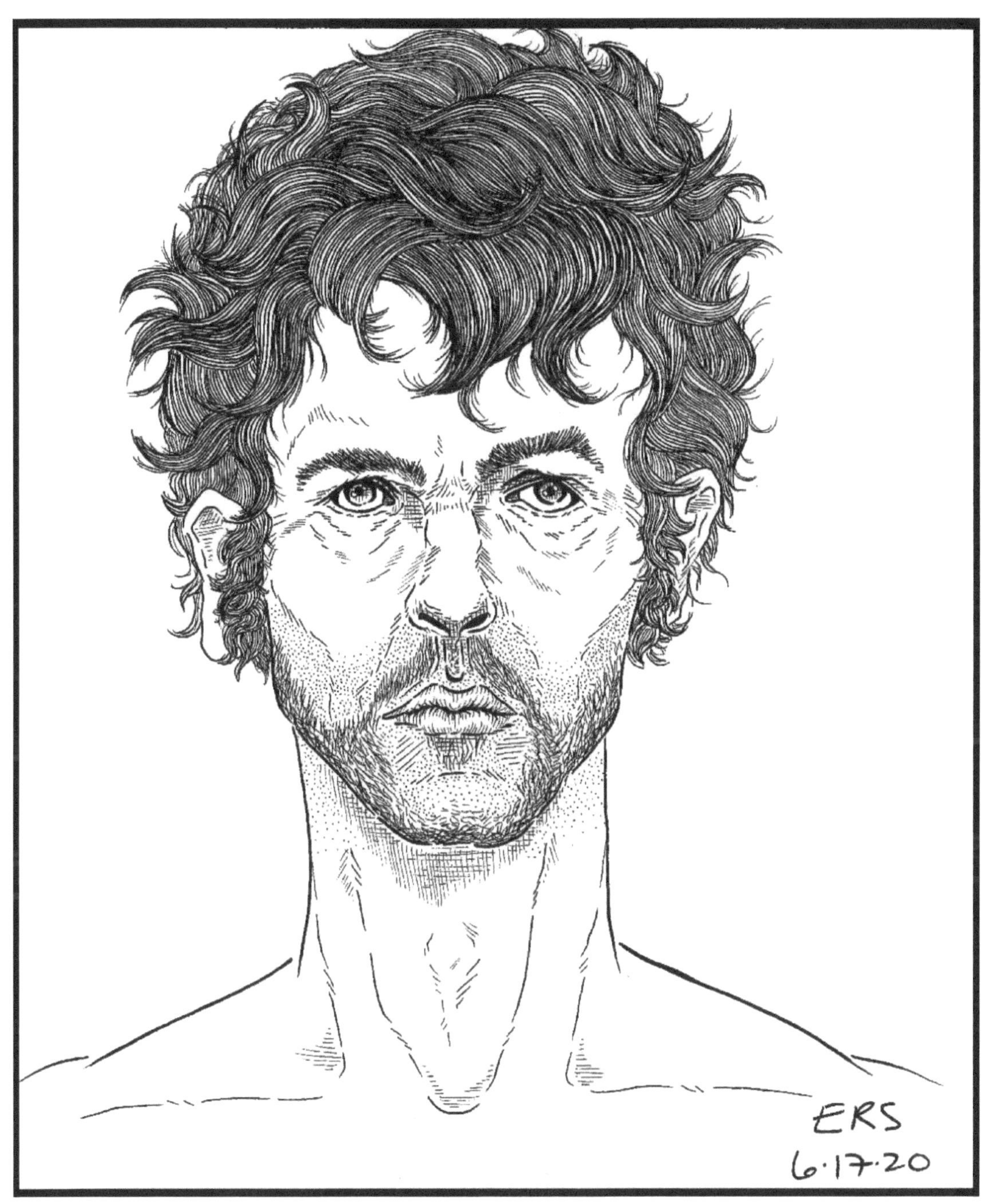

The Lover

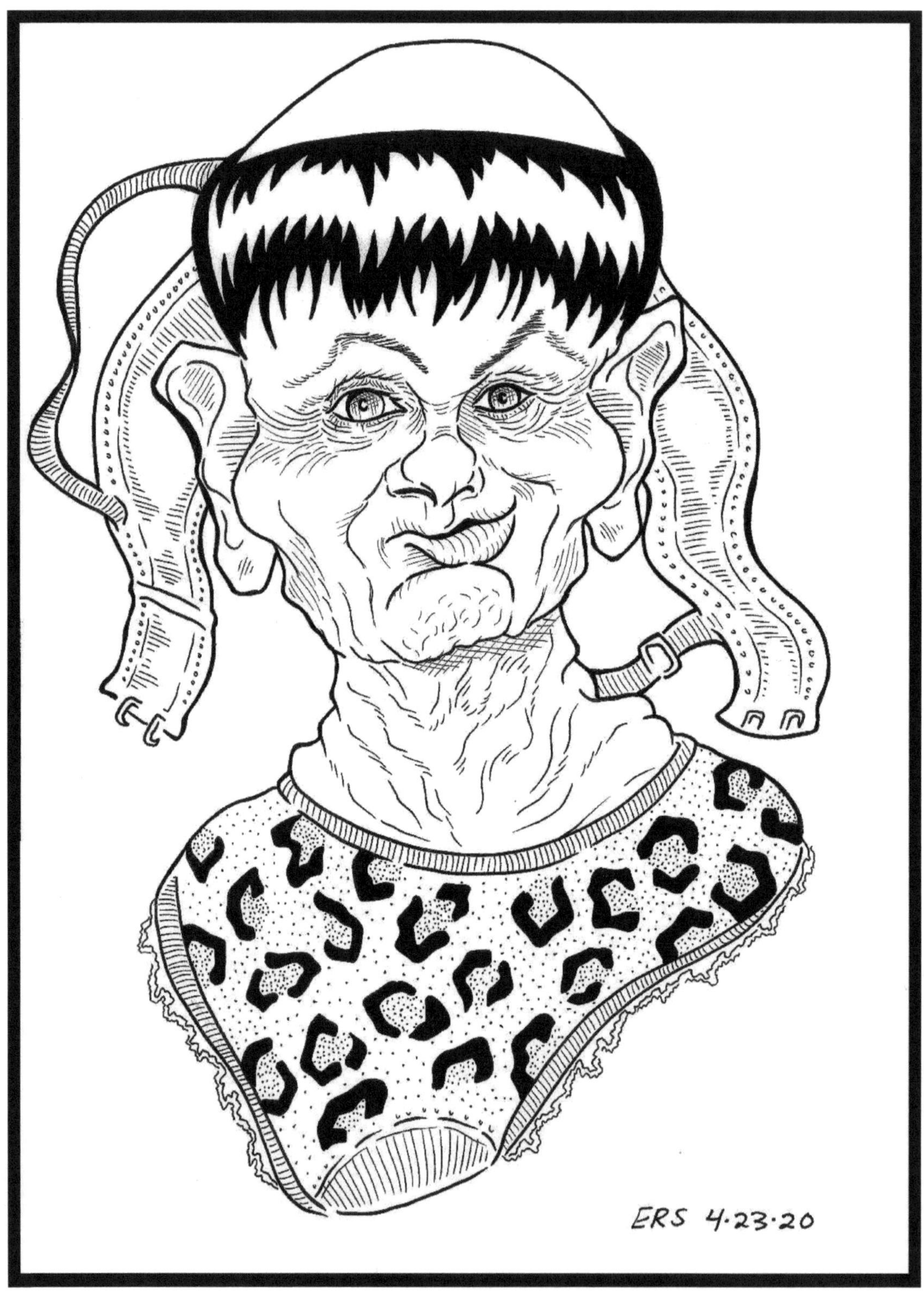

Licentious Monk

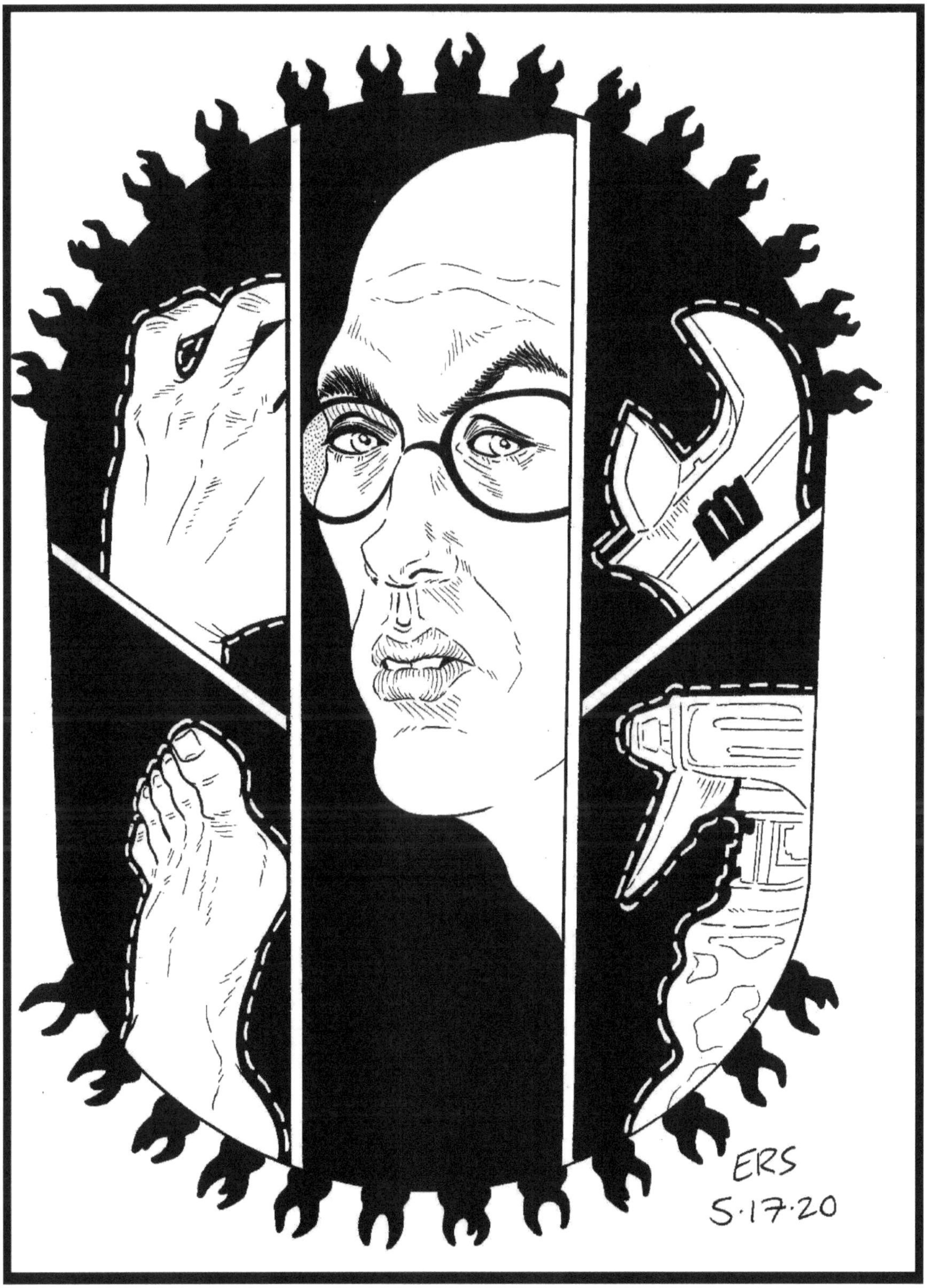

Mystery Neighbor

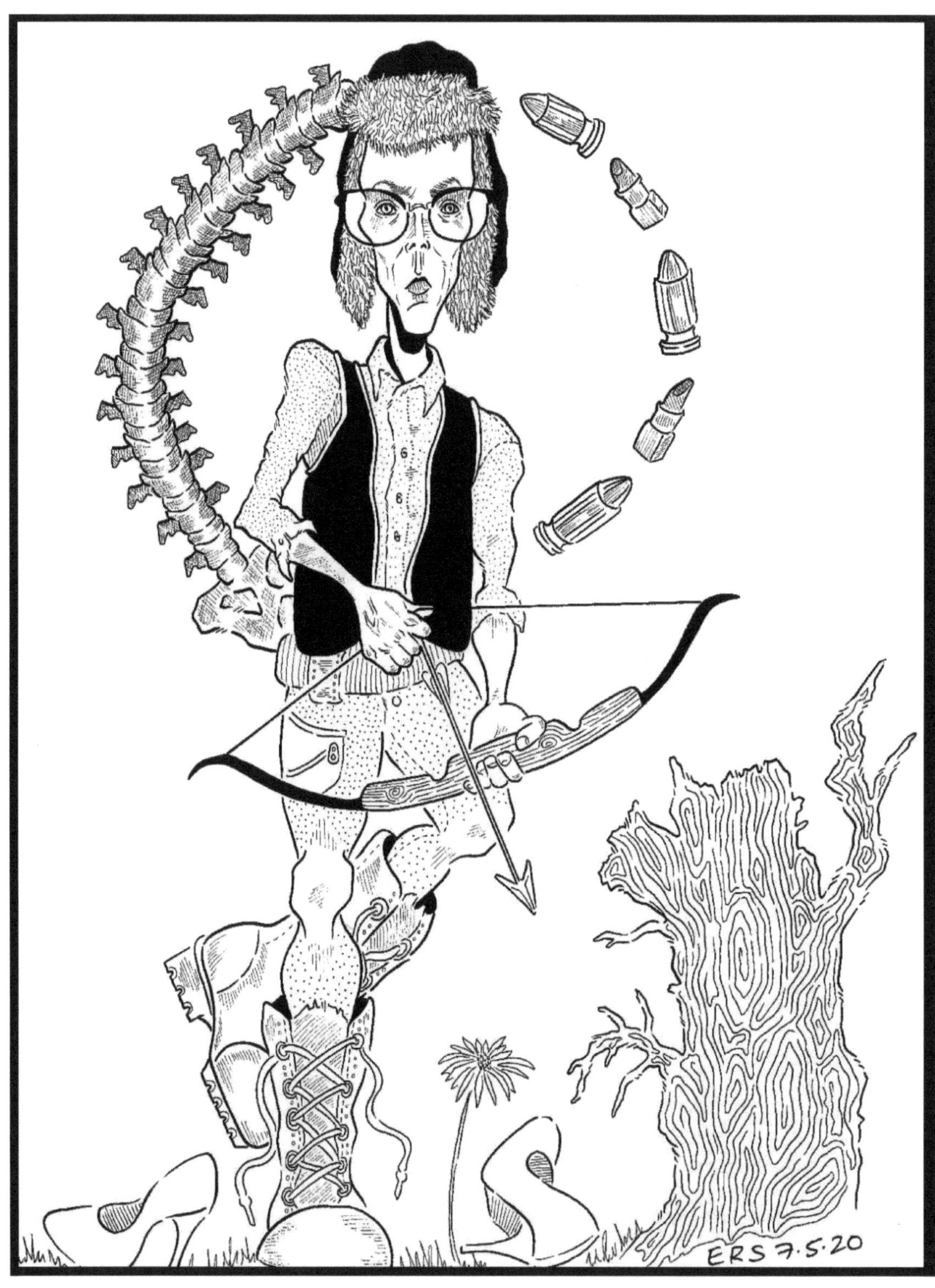

R. Hansen's Game

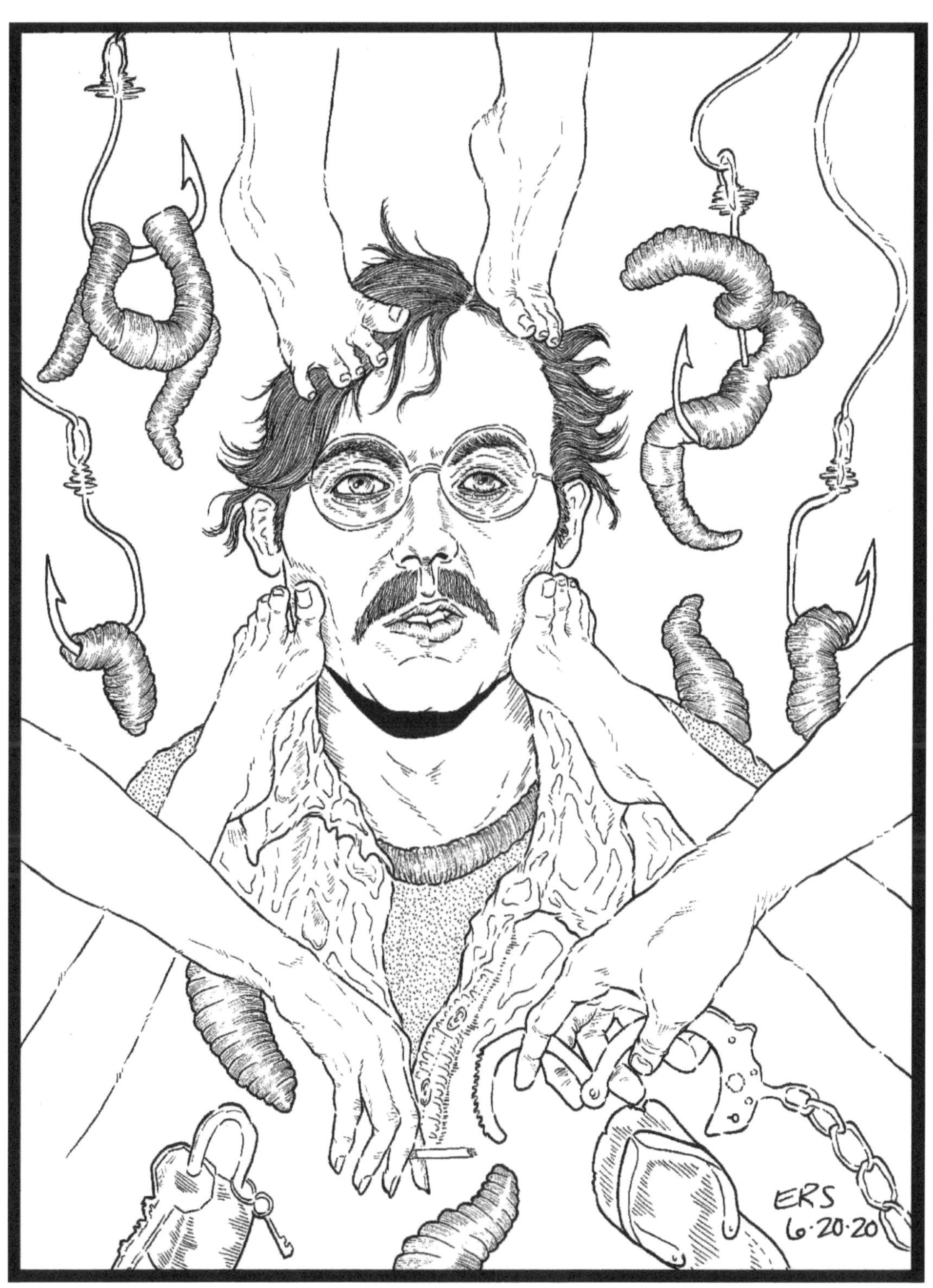

Keeping Company with Kemper

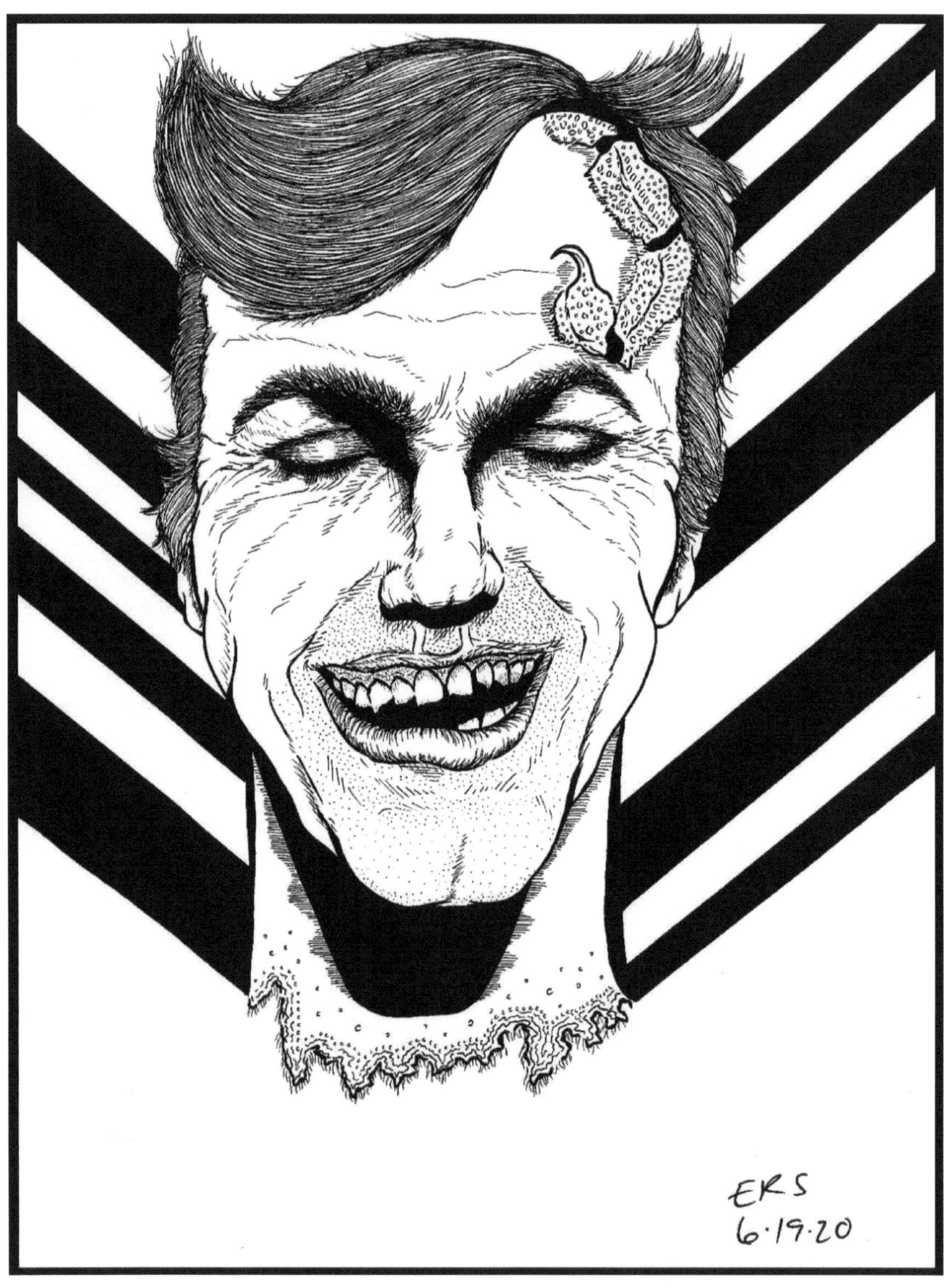

At Peace with Personal Demons

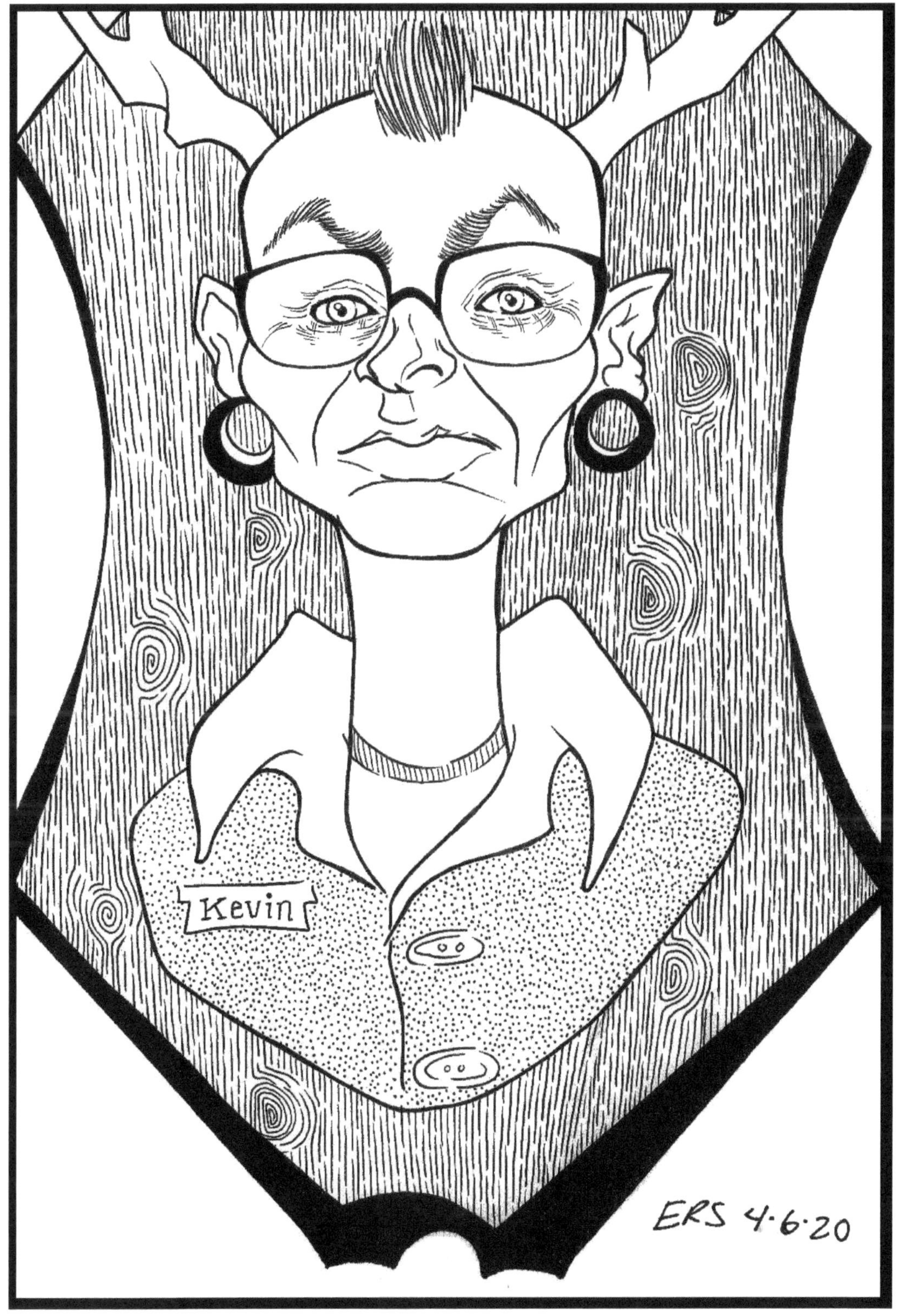

Essential Employee of the Month

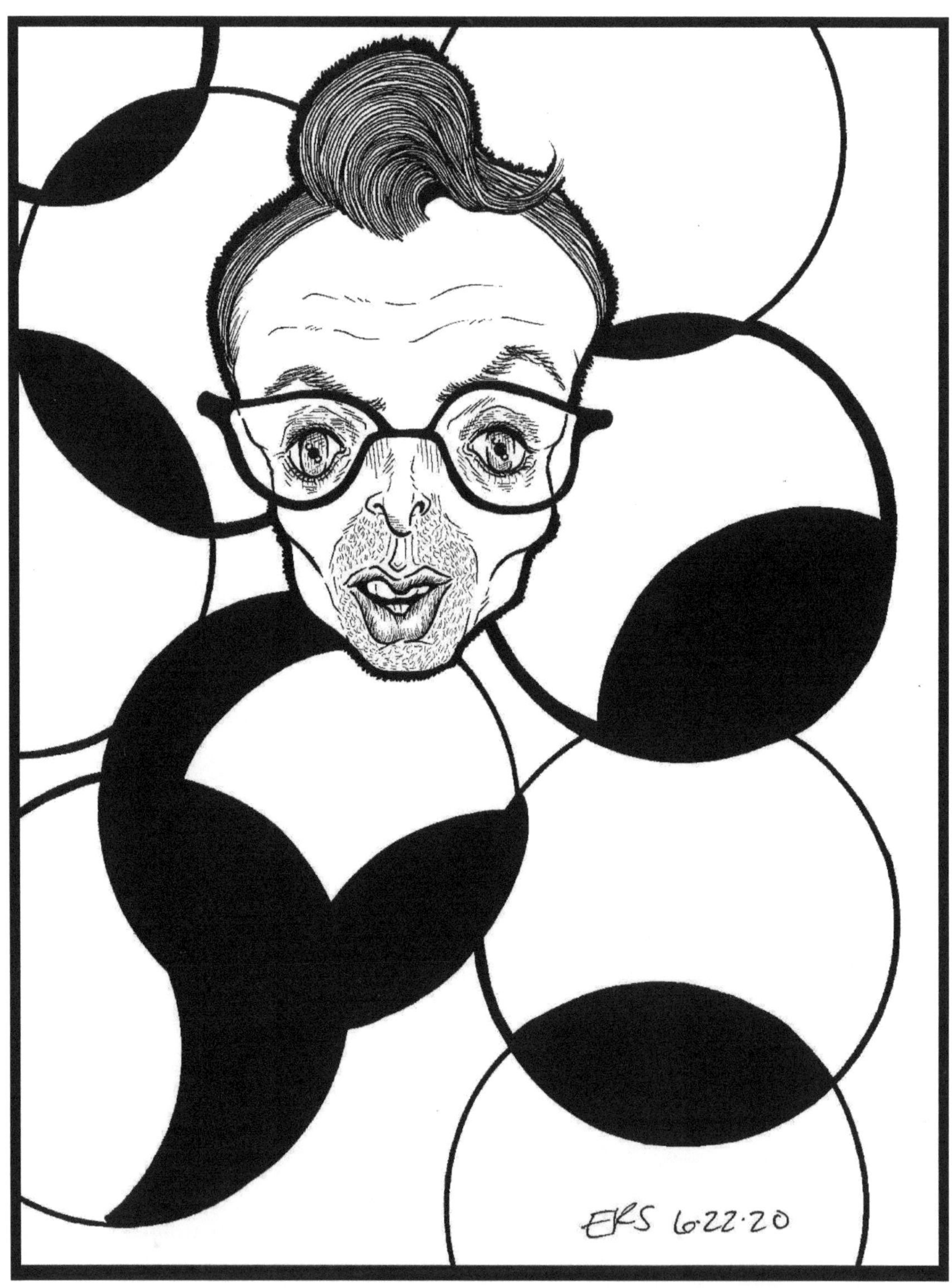

Unorthodox Psychiatrist

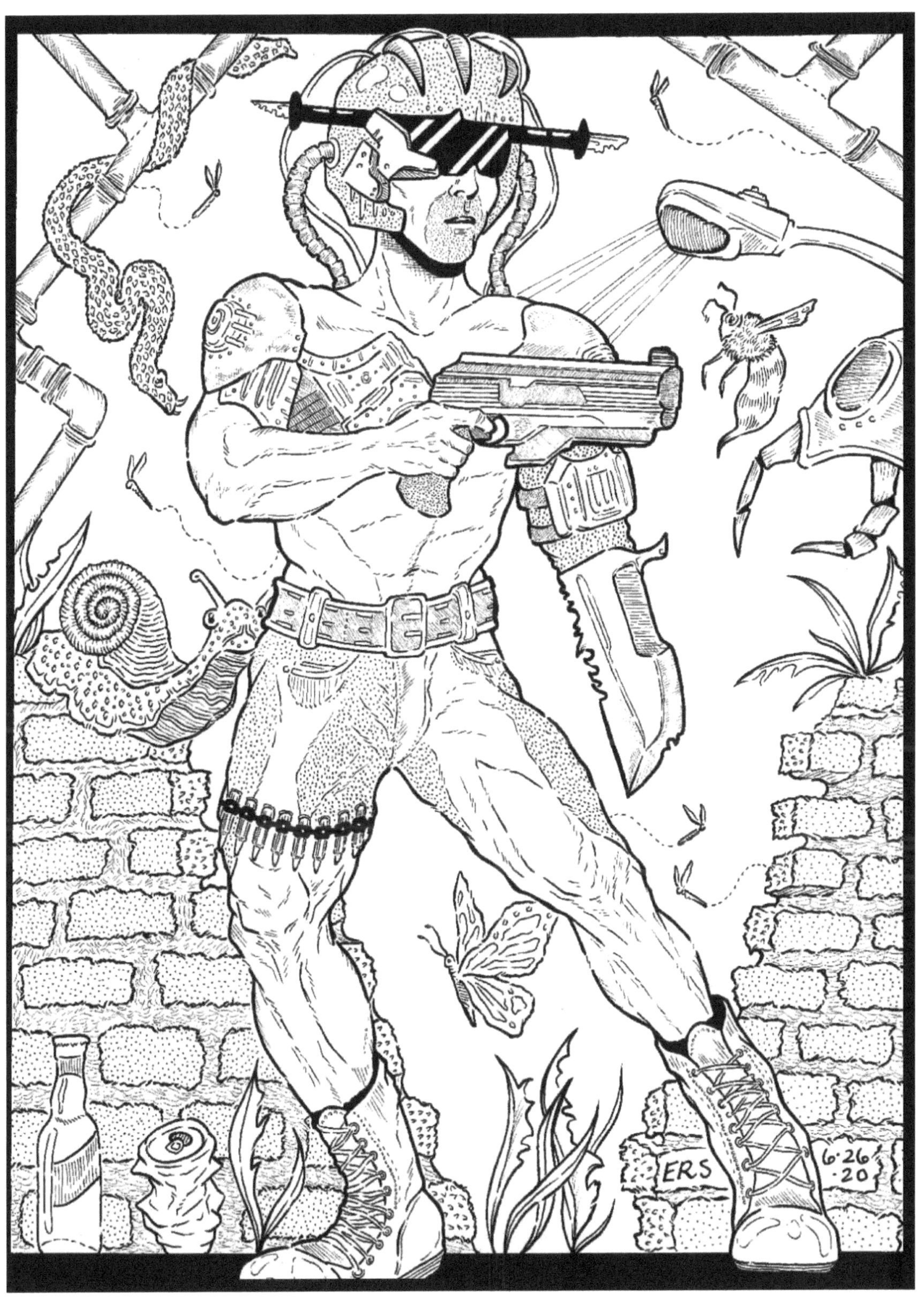

Solo Soldier

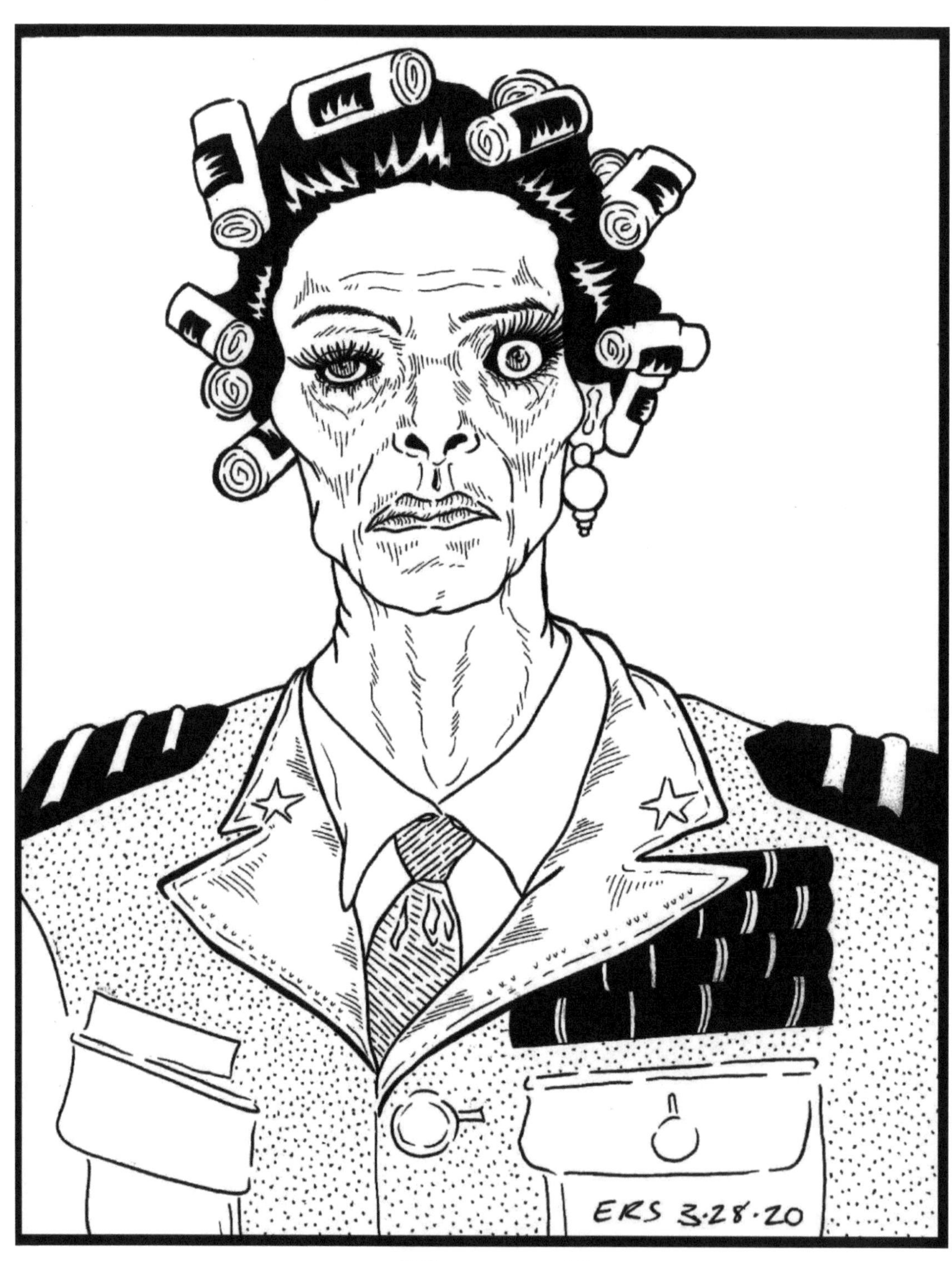

War on Drugs

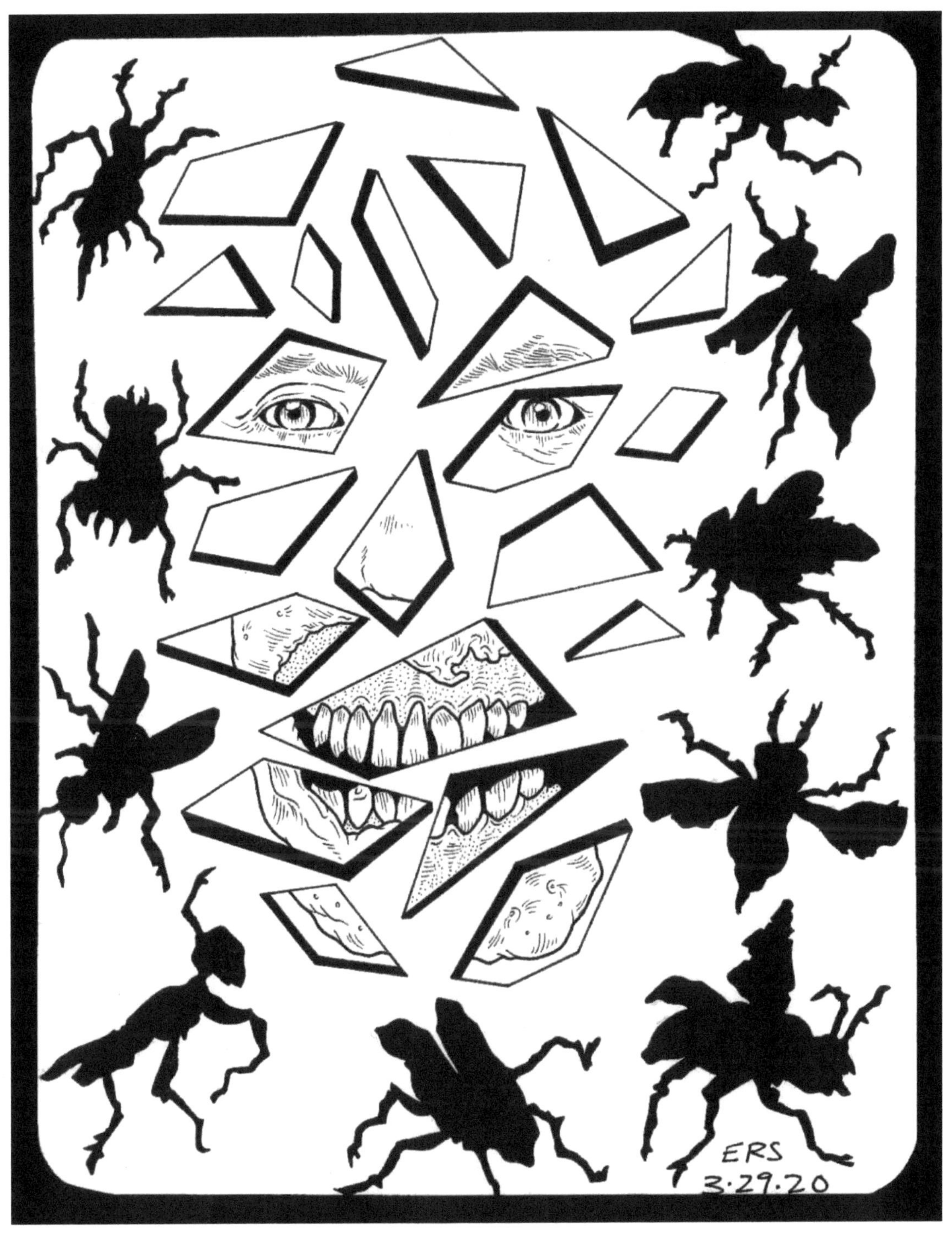

Fractured Identity

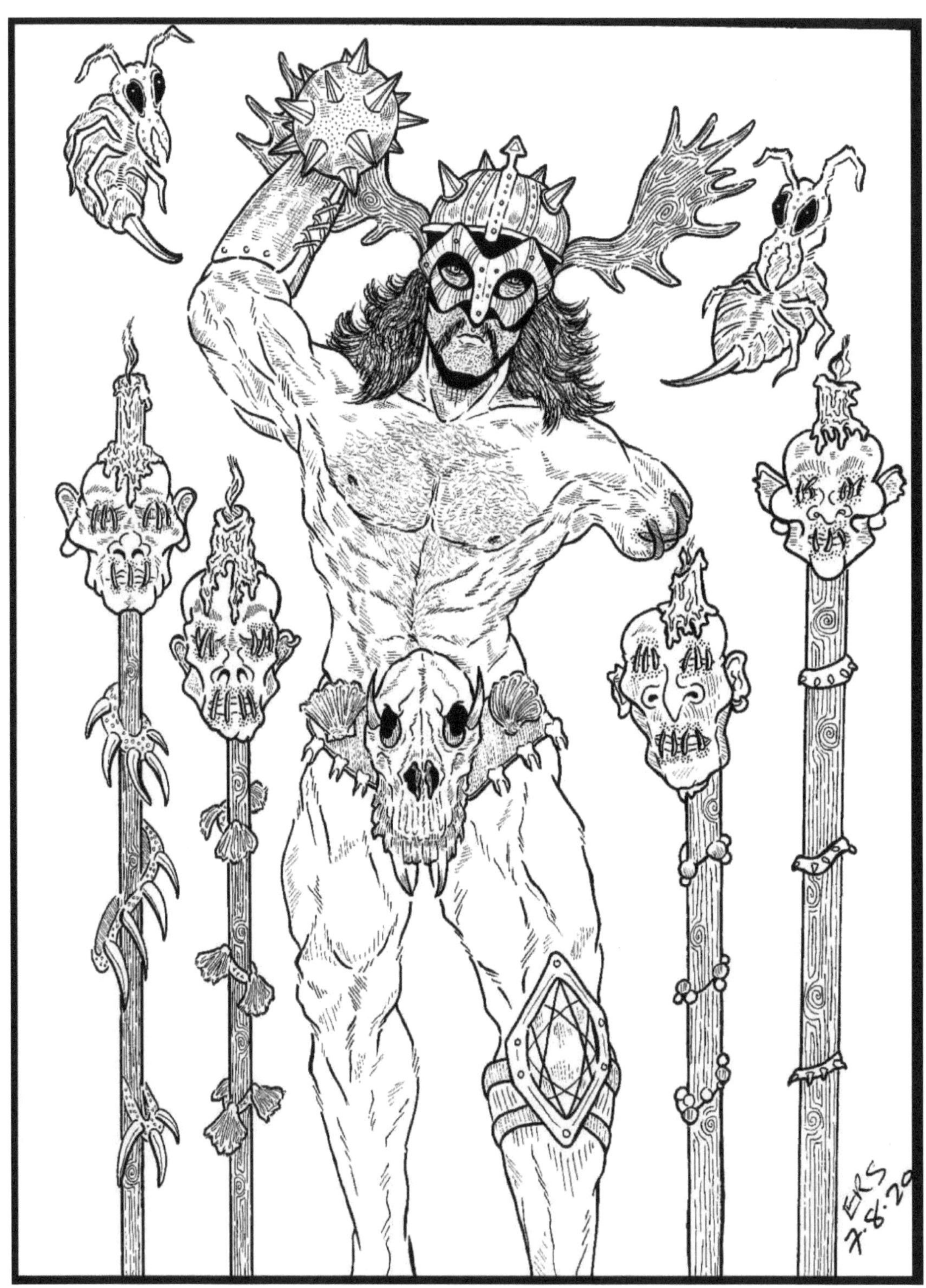

Antlos the Faithful

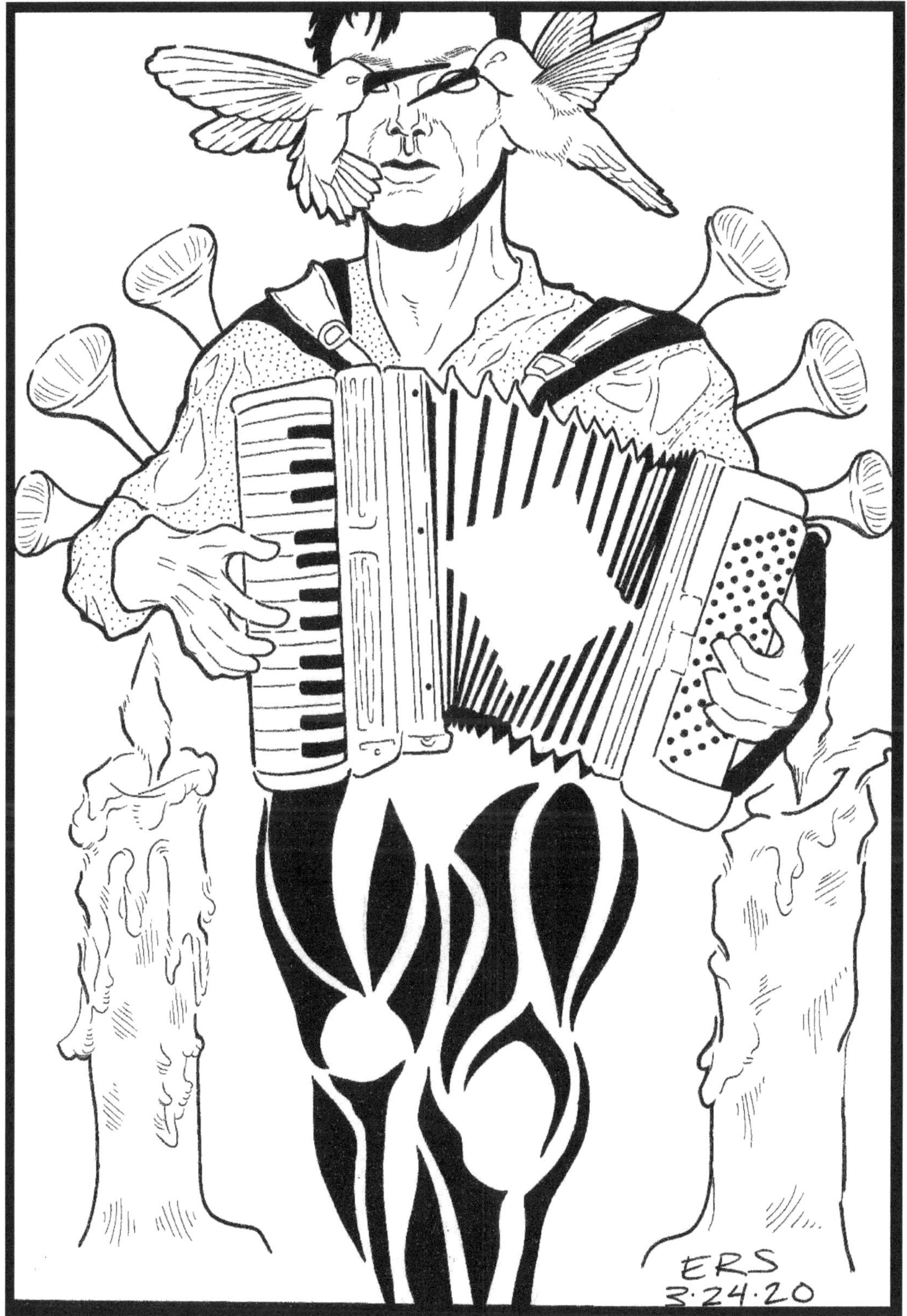

Plague Visions

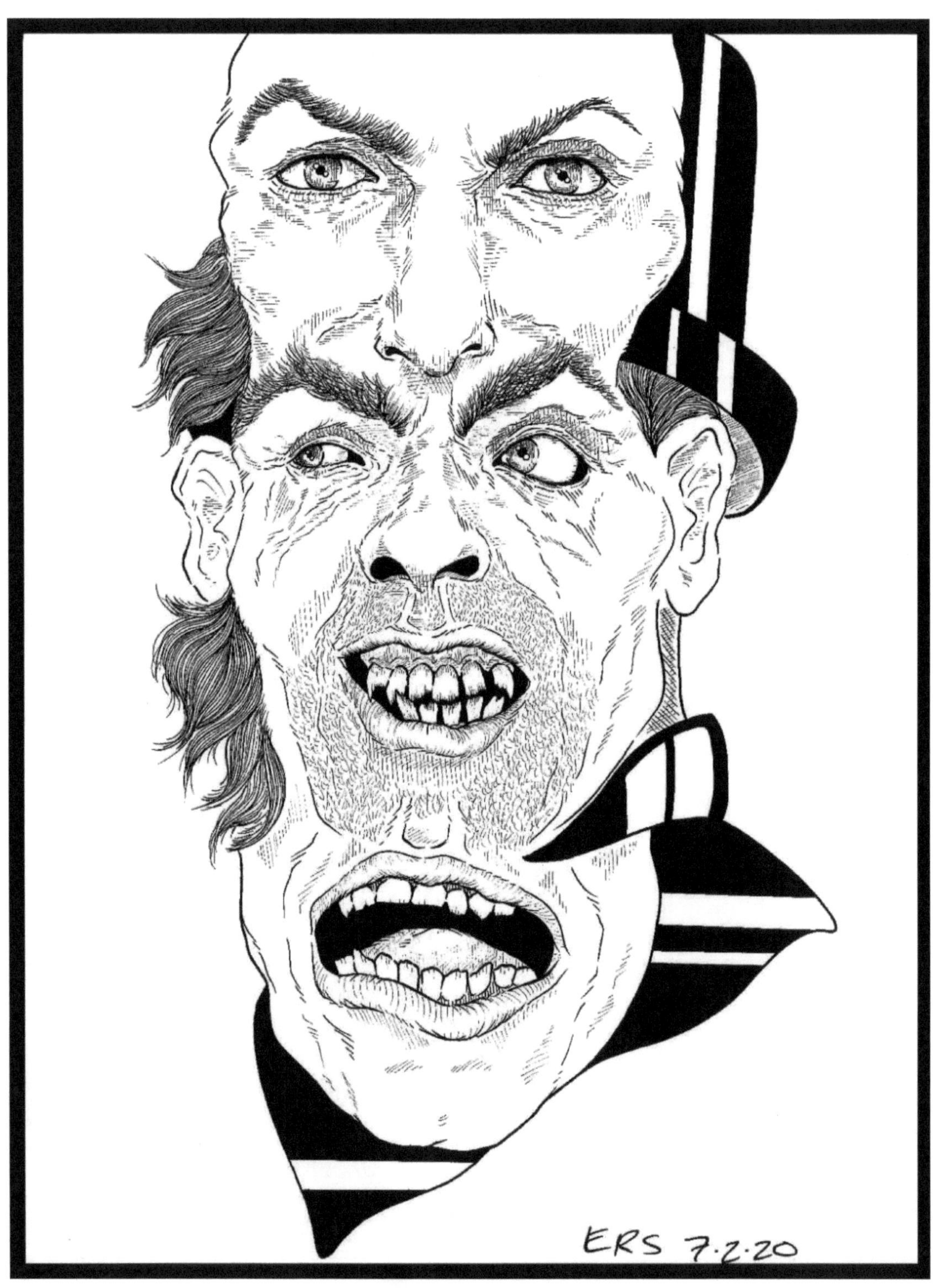

Hyde's Affair

IV. Fictive Kin

Abstract: Chapter Four

Clustered together, these personages form a necessary unit that play off each other. The situations that compel them to each other are circumspect, they only have themselves and those in dangerous proximity to answer aloud their daily anxieties and existential dilemmas. Relationships lingering behind the page, we may not know where they have been or where they may go, but in this moment they have chosen each other.

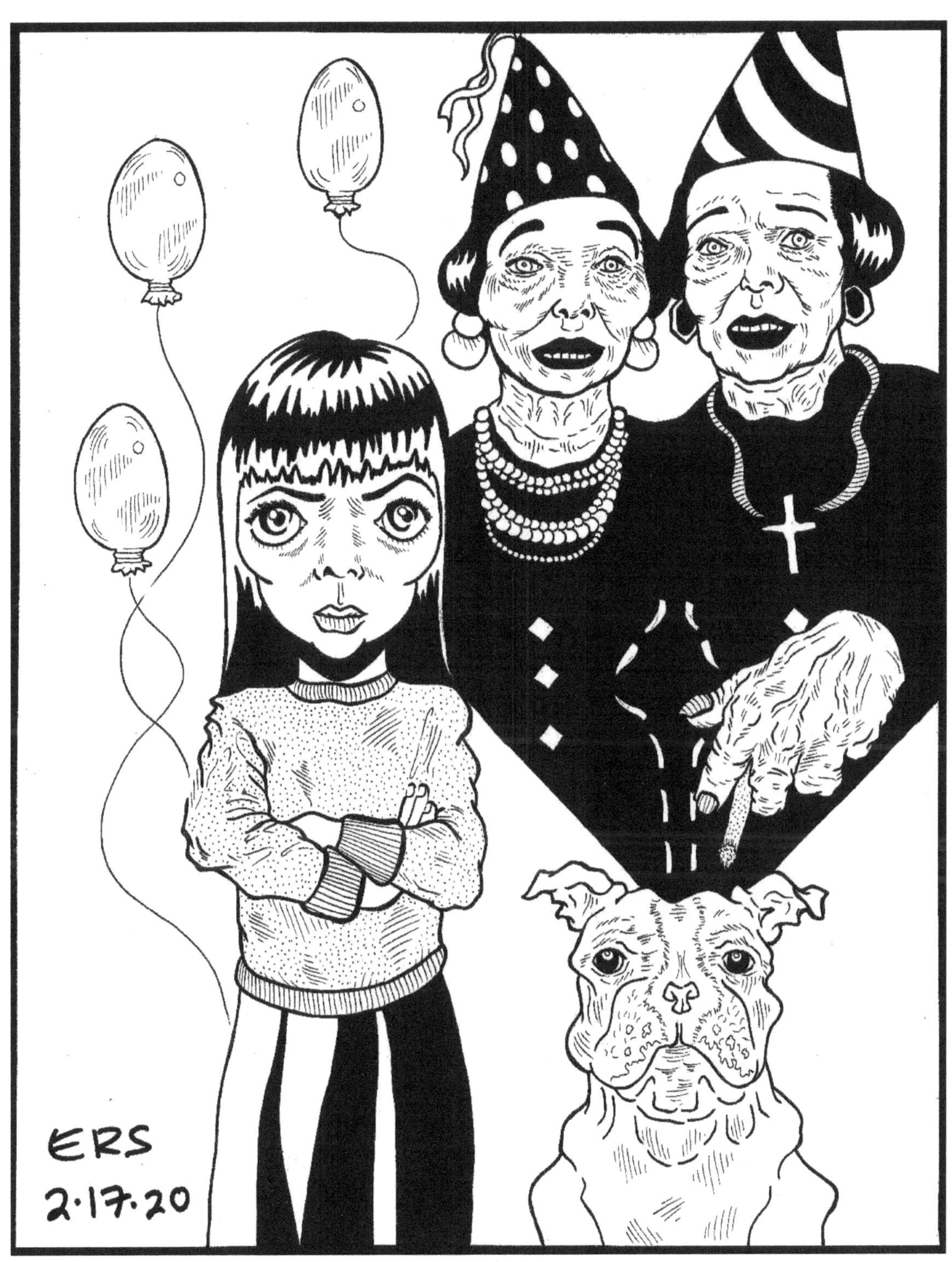

Birthday Brat

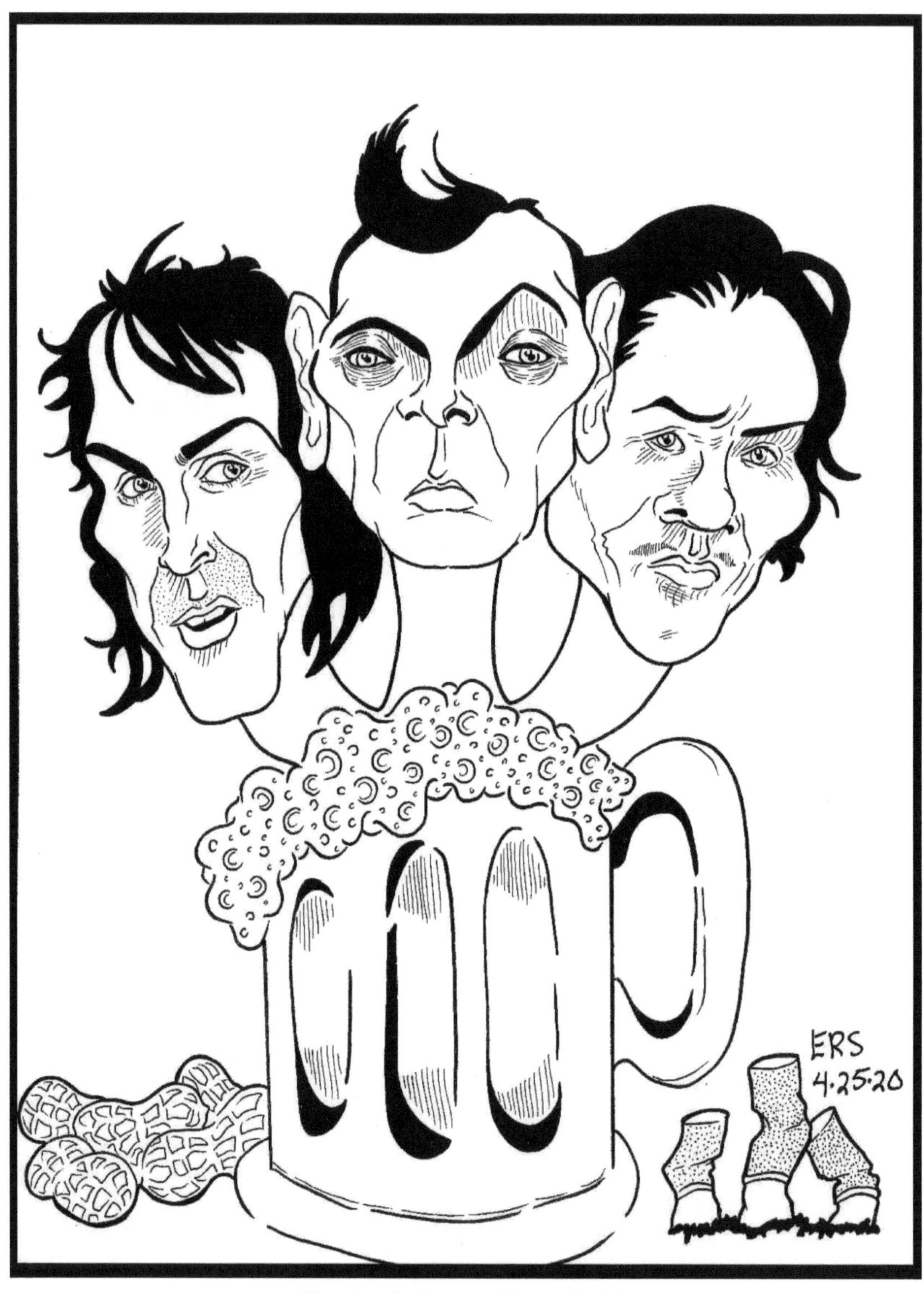

Drinking Buddies

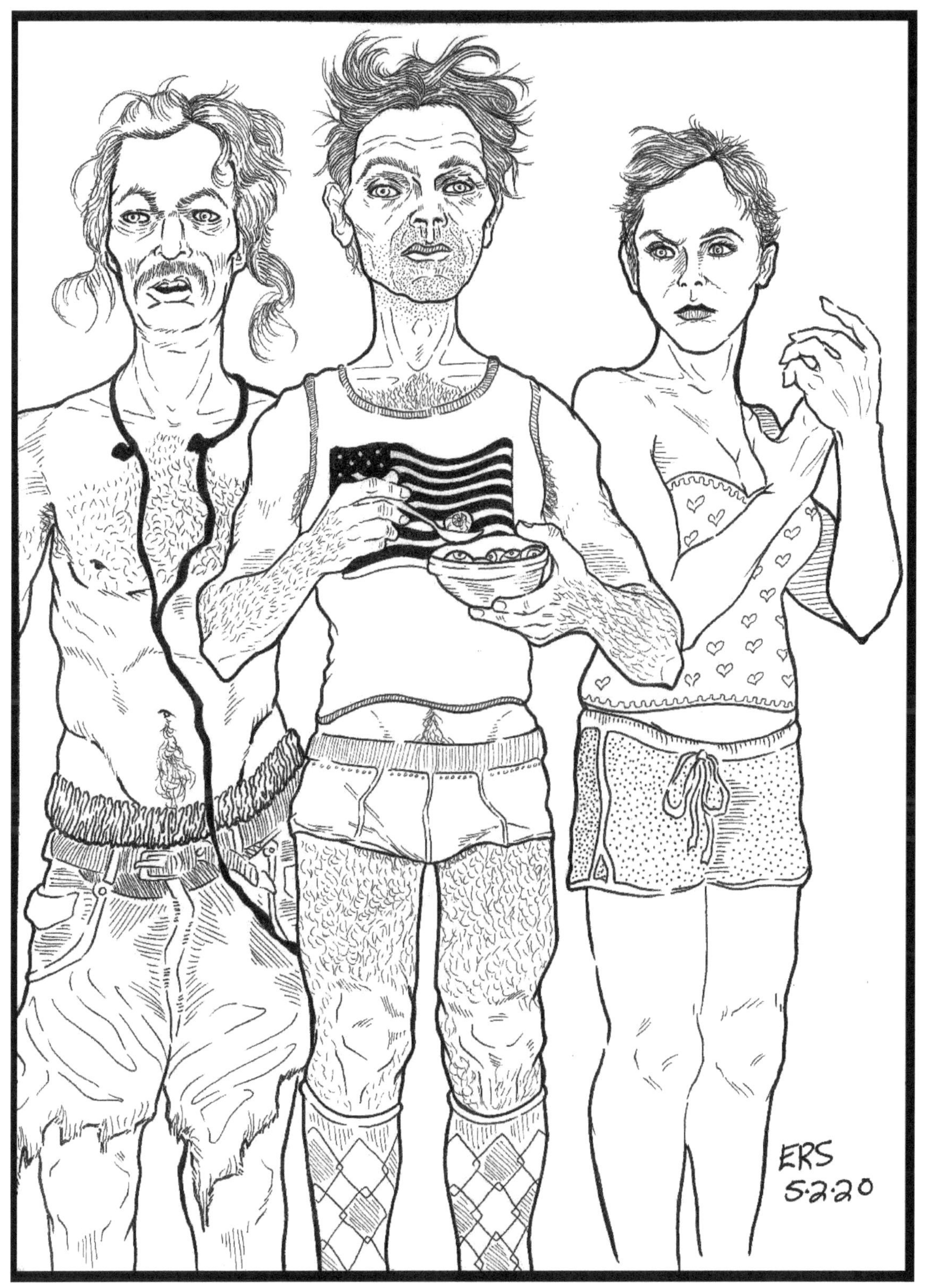

Shelter in Place

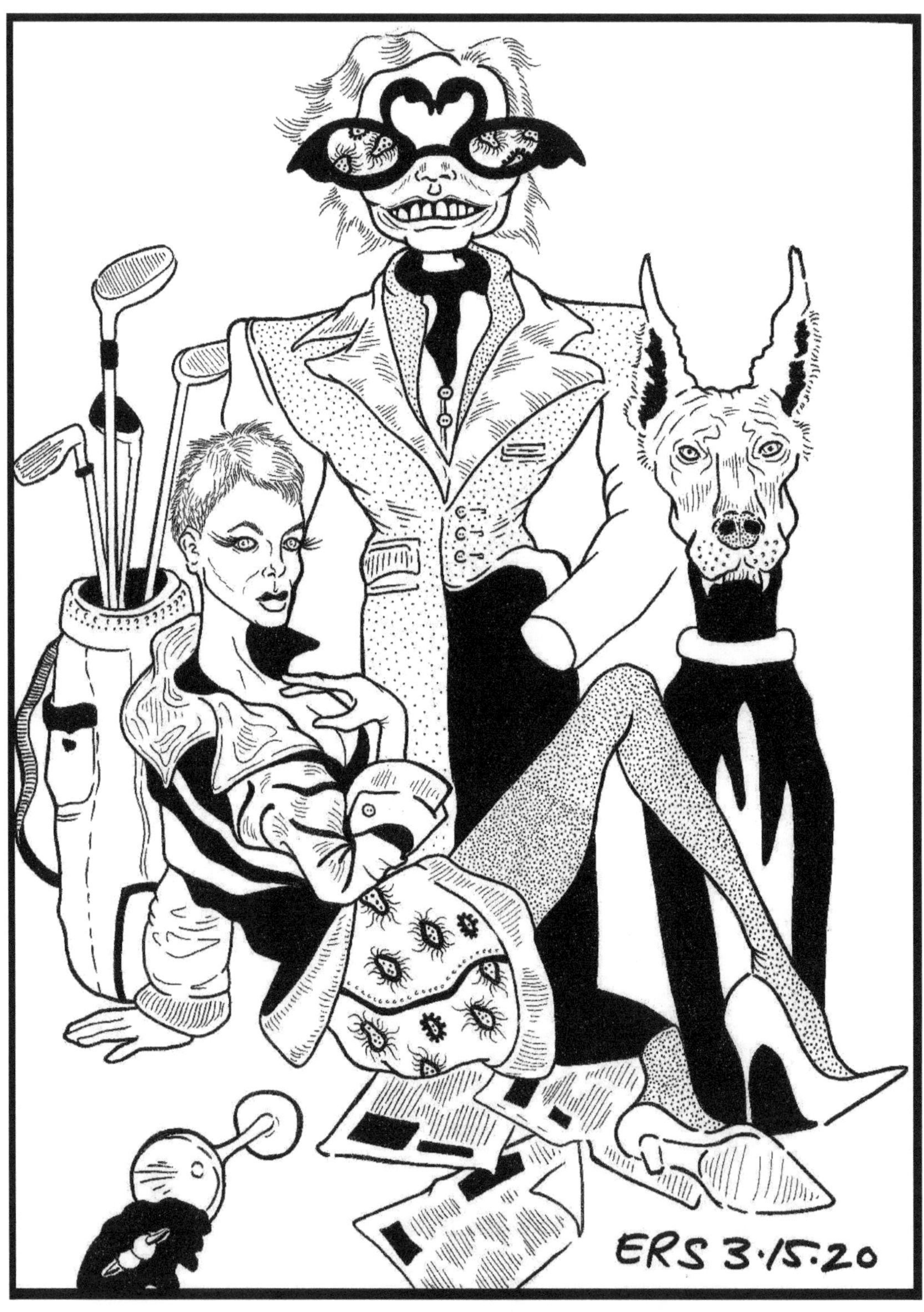

Mar-A-Lago Quarantine

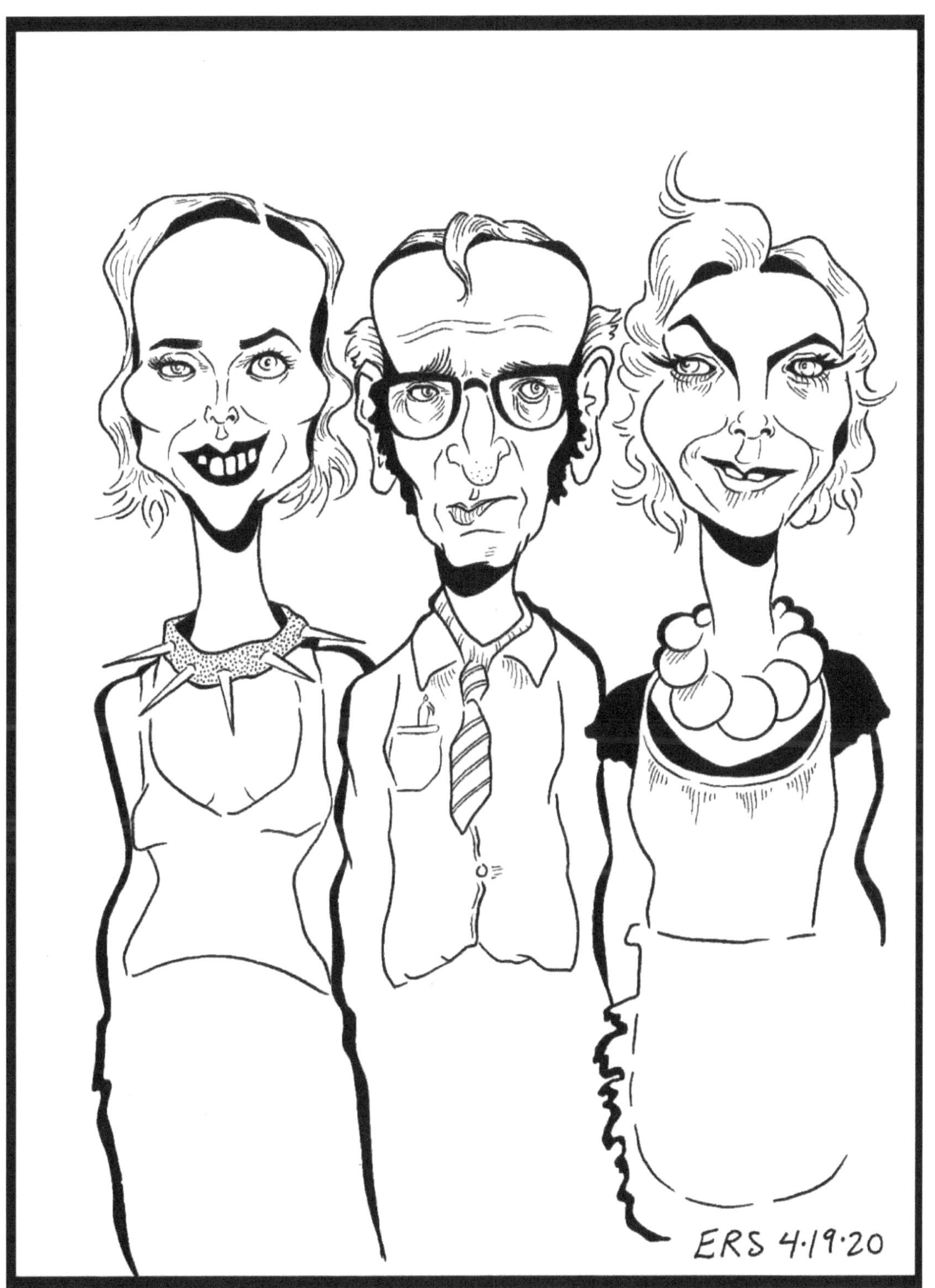

Graduation Barbecue

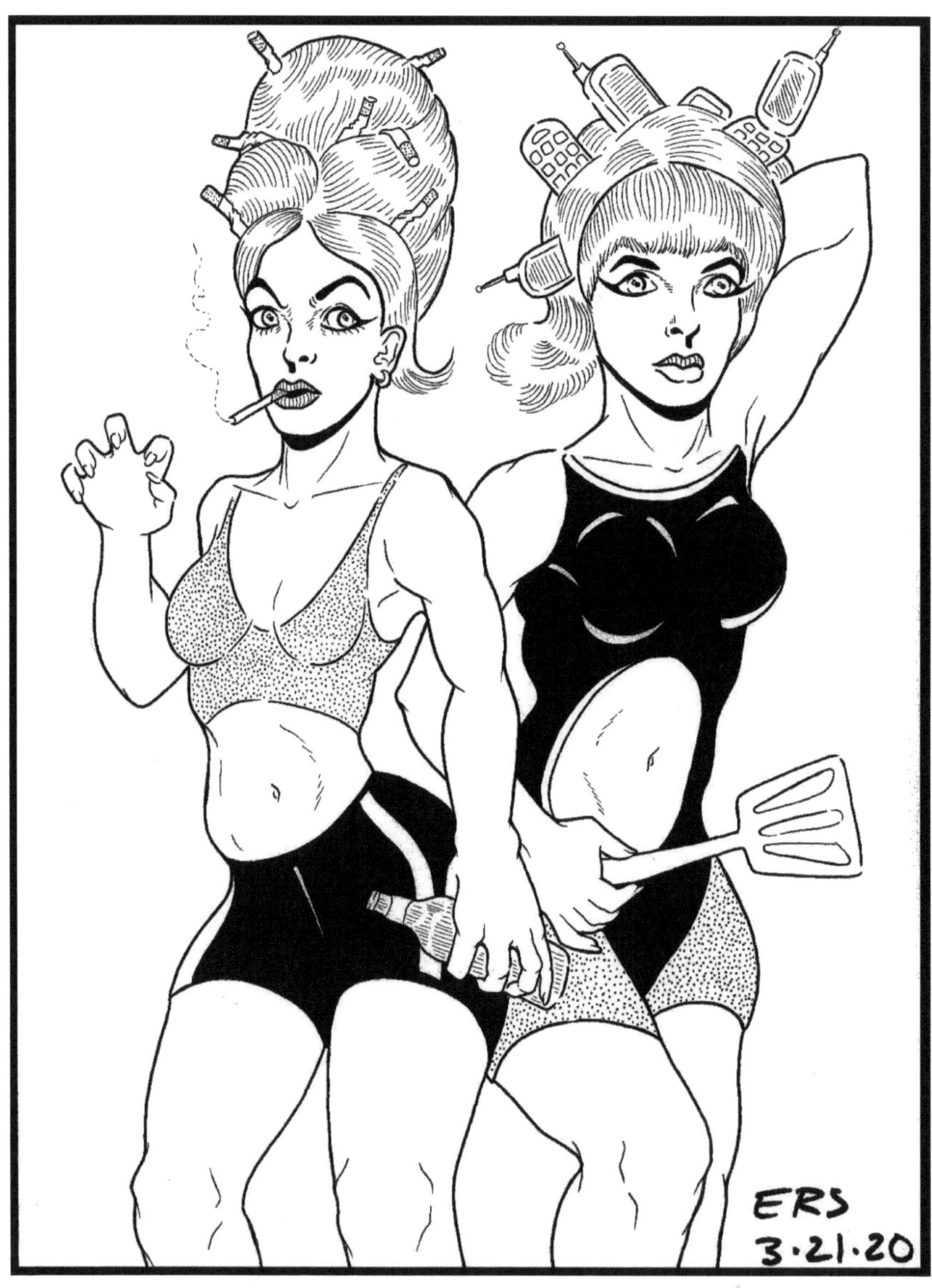

Barbies that Eat Arby's

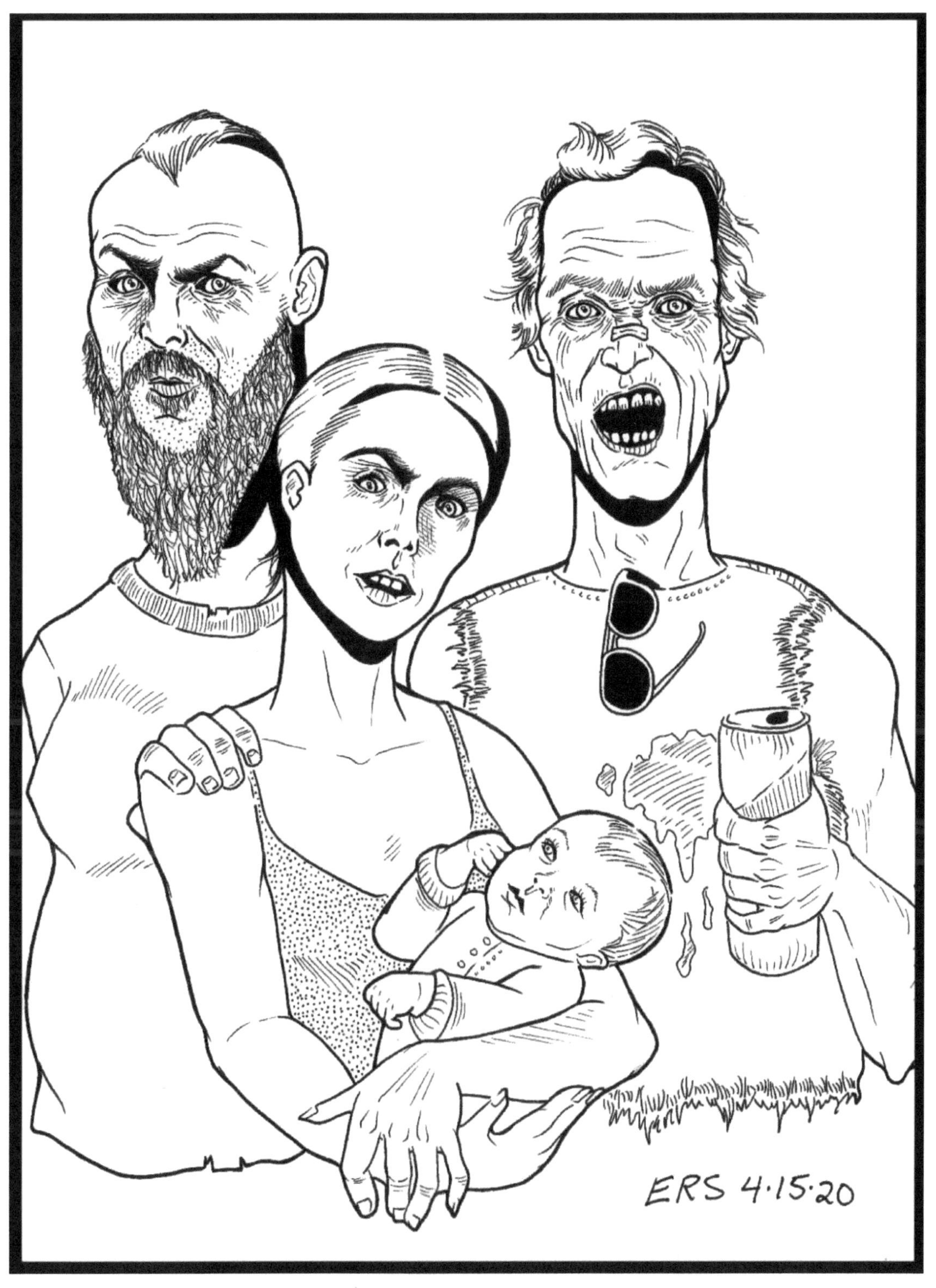

Provincial Family Portrait